COACH K

BUILDING THE DUKE DYNASTY

The Story of
Mike Krzyzewski
and the
Winning Tradition at
Duke University

By Gregg Doyel

ADDAX
PUBLISHING
GROUP

LENEXA, KS

Published by Addax Publishing Group, Inc.
Copyright © 1999 by Gregg Doyel
Edited by An Beard
Designed by Laura Bolter
Cover Designed by Laura Bolter

ISBN: 1-886110-86-7

Printed in the USA

1 3 5 7 9 10 8 6 4 2

COACH K

BUILDING THE
DUKE DYNASTY

The Story of
Mike Krzyzewski
and the
Winning Tradition at
Duke University

By Gregg Doyel

DEDICATION

For my little boy Jackson, who, bless his heart, slept every afternoon for two hours, and my older little boy Macon, who stoically watched *Balto* at the same time, and my wife Melody, who patiently played center field and handled everything hit from foul pole to foul pole.

TABLE OF CONTENTS

ACKNOWLEDGMENTS

So many people made writing this first book so much smoother than it could, and probably should, have gone. A whole host of people from *The Charlotte Observer* gave their time and talent to this non-Observer project, most notably the pro bono work of librarians Marion Paynter, Sara Klemmer and Ann Bryant (photos), who were equal parts helpful and patient. Not an easy balance, for sure. Thanks also to Susan Gilbert for freeing up so many pictures, Davie Hinshaw for finding the right ones, and all the photogs who shot them in the first place, plus Mark Hames for having good hands when the computer on which this book was written crashed.

Thanks to those who came earlier in *The Observer's* Raleigh bureau, namely Charles Chandler and Rick Bonnell, and also Scott Fowler, Tom Sorensen and the sports writers Green, Ron and Ron Jr., for chronicling so well Duke's recent history. In the same vein, thanks to authors John Feinstein (*A March to Madness*), Joe Menzer (*Four Corners*) and Bill Brill with Mike Krzyzewski (*A Season is a Lifetime*).

9

Thanks to Joe Drape of *The New York Times,* whose poolside advice was stronger even than the margaritas, and to the aforementioned Menzer of *The Winston-Salem Journal,* who also gave solid advice (but no margaritas).

Thanks to sports information specialists Mike Cragg of Duke and Brian Morrison of the Atlantic Coast Conference for all that good sports information.

Thanks to An Beard and the rest of the people at Addax for providing this opportunity, and to *Observer* bosses Gary Schwab and Harry Pickett for the go-ahead.

And a special thanks to Nick Valvano and all the Duke players and coaches, past and present, who gave unselfishly of their time.

INTRODUCTION

March 29, 1999.
Seven forty-six p.m.
St. Petersburg, Florida.

The massive bus cuts through the game-day traffic and rolls down a ramp and underneath Tropicana Field, where immortality awaits. Slowly the Duke basketball team disembarks and enters the gigantic, domed baseball stadium that is the site of the 1999 Final Four. The national championship is there for the taking tonight, and the Blue Devils saunter toward their destiny, dressed in all black, their stone faces a mixture of anger and arrogance. The only Duke player who makes a sound is National Player of the Year, Elton Brand, the 6-foot-8, 265-pound sophomore center, who nods his head and echoes the sounds coming from his compact disc headphones. This reeks of being Duke's night, right down to the royal blue hue of the temporary carpet that carries the players toward their locker room and, soon enough, onto the Tropicana Field floor to face Connecticut.

Mike Krzyzewski is the last to leave the bus. The Duke coach sits in the second row, next to his wife, Mickie, and there he stays as his players and assistants and support personnel file off the bus. Krzyzewski doesn't say a word to them as they leave. They are silent, too.

After the bus empties, Krzyzewski hoists himself out of his seat, no easy trick for a man who will have a degenerating hip surgically replaced in six days, and steps off the bus. He hugs his three daughters, youngest to oldest: Jamie, 17; Lindy, 21; and Debbie, 28. Krzyzewski turns to his wife, wraps his arms around her, and receives a kiss for luck. Then he follows that royal blue carpet into the locker room.

Still he hasn't said a word.

The words will come later. In the end they will be words of consolation, words of disappointment. This Duke team, which some feel is Krzyzewski's best in nineteen seasons at Duke – better even than the back-to-back national championship teams of 1991 and 1992 – finds itself in only its third down-to-the-wire game of the season. The first time, in November at the Carrs Great Alaska Shootout, the Blue Devils lose 77-75 to Cincinnati on a dunk near the buzzer. The second time, in January against St. John's, the Blue Devils are taken to overtime but win even with the All-American Brand on the bench with five fouls.

Now this. Duke is the monster of the 1998-99 college basketball season, entering the national title game with a 37-1 record, but Connecticut stands up to the monster, even petulantly flicks it in the nose a time or two during the course of the game, and when the horn sounds for the last time, the scoreboard reads like a misprint:

Connecticut 77, Duke 74.

More than forty thousand people are making painfully loud noise in the stands, and the Connecticut team is making even more painful noise on the court. This was to be a coronation not only for the Duke team, which would have taken its place among the best of all time with a victory, but also for Krzyzewski, who would have become the first coach since UCLA's masterful John Wooden nearly a quarter-century earlier to win three national titles in the same decade.

As the crowd buzzes in amazed appreciation at what it has just witnessed, and as the Huskies run manic sprints around the court, and as the rest of the Blue Devils plod down the royal blue carpet toward their crypt of a locker room, Duke point guard William Avery remains on the court, surrounded by the last gasps of March Madness. Surrounded by celebrating Connecticut players, Avery stands on the court, crying and alone.

On his way to the locker room, Krzyzewski spots Avery, a sensitive sophomore who three years earlier had to make a near-miraculous recovery in the classroom as a high school senior to meet Duke's stringent academic requirements and fulfill his dream of playing for Krzyzewski. Avery, now one of the best point guards in the country, has played a sub-par game, and he knows it. No doubt Krzyzewski knows it, too.

Krzyzewski sticks his chin out and forges a path through the Connecticut celebration over to Avery, grabs him around the shoulders, pulls him close and pats the back of his head. And then Krzyzewski starts to talk.

"It's all right, William. It's all right."

———

Chapter One

HIP CHIC

Mike Krzyzewski's left hip is gone, a casualty of too much coaching, too many media interviews, too many autographs, too many speaking engagements. Too much, for too long. And so, like a demon exorcised from an otherwise pure man, the left hip had to go. It went at a most fitting time – exactly six days after Duke ended its 1998-99 season with a loss to Connecticut in the national championship game, an ending that was horribly disappointing to Krzyzewski in one sense, for his team was a nearly 10-point favorite to beat the Huskies for the NCAA title, yet in another sense an ending that was incredibly fulfilling.

Duke was all the way back. Coach K, too.

Some details at the periphery of the surgery itself are proof of that. People in other parts of the country, even hard-core college basketball fans, probably cannot conceive of the magnitude of Atlantic Coast Conference basketball in general, and Duke basketball in particular, in the state of North Carolina. Fans of Duke call newspaper reporters at home to complain about a bias toward the

University of North Carolina. Fans of North Carolina call those same reporters and complain about a bias toward Duke. Fans of N.C. State also call, complaining about a bias toward everyone else. Round and round it goes, because, in the state of North Carolina, ACC and Duke basketball are bigger than NASCAR. Bigger than tobacco.

And bigger, apparently, than hip replacement surgery.

When news surfaced in February of the 1998-99 season that Krzyzewski would have his left hip replaced after the season, other patients in the Raleigh-Durham-Chapel Hill area who faced the same procedure began clamoring to have their hip replacement performed at the same hospital on the same day. Facing a painful procedure that would see the removal, and replacement, of one of the bigger bones in their body, all these people seemed to care about was having it done as closely as possible to Krzyzewski. Afterward, supposedly, they wanted to lie in bed, pain-killered up, next to the Duke coach.

Krzyzewski and hospital officials got around that potential nuisance by pulling a fast one on the rest of the hip-transplant world, not to mention the media – sneaking Krzyzewski into the hospital 24 hours early and performing the procedure in glorious anonymity.

Because Duke basketball is big. And Coach K, impossibly, is somehow even bigger. Two days before the surgery, *The Durham Herald-Sun* and *The Raleigh News & Observer* ran front-page stories quoting Duke and hospital representatives who were pleading for Krzyzewski's privacy. The hospital announced it would set up a web page on the Internet for the sole purpose of providing daily updates on the success of Krzyzewski's surgery, and then his recovery.

"The family is asking for the fewest possible interruptions," a hospital spokesman said.

Interruptions. That's a pretty good word for what

drove Krzyzewski onto a surgeon's table in 1999 – and very nearly out of coaching four and a half years earlier. For too many years he had spent too much energy being Coach K, when what he really needed to be was Mike to his wife, Daddy to his three daughters, and Coach to his players. That's all. But that wasn't enough for Coach K, and it sure wasn't enough for everyone around him.

The hip replacement surgery after the 1999 national championship game, that was a metaphor. Krzyzewski wasn't just disposing of the thing that connects his leg bone to his back bone, a thing that in his case was causing daily, excruciating pain. He was disposing of a ghost from 1994, a remnant of a time when he nearly crashed, and the Duke basketball dynasty nearly crashed along with him. Don't think dynasties can collapse? Ask once-sturdy programs like N.C. State, Kentucky and Georgetown, which went from national powerhouses in the 1970s and 1980s to regional mediocrity in a matter of a few years (though Kentucky has bounced back just as dramatically).

The hip was, once fifth-year senior Trajan Langdon used up his eligibility and played his final collegiate game in the 1999 Final Four, the last link to that dreadful 1994-95 season. The hip was the last painful reminder to Krzyzewski of what had gone wrong, and why.

The hip had to go. For more than medical reasons.

Duke had been at the pinnacle of college basketball. And then ...

"A whole bunch of things were just taken away," Krzyzewski said.

Duke basketball was just so mammoth, especially since Krzyzewski had arrived in 1980-81. In the next nineteen seasons, Duke had gone 469-155, with forty-eight NCAA tournament victories, eight Final Four appearances and two national championships. Almost a full calendar year – fifty-one weeks, spread from 1986 to 1999 – had passed with Duke ranked No. 1 in the country. A seat in Cameron Indoor Stadium, which seats 9,314 people, most of them rabid Duke students, was the toughest ticket in town, and Krzyzewski was considered among the top coaches in college basketball. He was named National Coach of the Year six times: in 1986, 1989, 1991, 1992, 1997 and 1999.

In the middle of that nineteen-year string of dominance was one nine-year stretch of total absurdity. From 1986 to 1994, the Blue Devils reached the Final Four seven times in nine years. It was an insanely successful run, something that had been done only once before, by John Wooden's brilliant UCLA teams of the 1960s and early 1970s featuring Bill Walton and Lew Alcindor (before he changed his name to Kareem Abdul-Jabbar). Other than Duke, no program has gone to seven Final Fours in nine years since those Bruins. Other than Duke, no program has come close. Connecticut, the 1999 national champions, had never been to the Final Four before, not even once. And the Huskies entered the 1998-99 season roundly considered one of the most consistently excellent programs of the late 1980s and 1990s.

Seven Final Fours in nine years. That's what Duke did. That's what Krzyzewski did.

"Getting to the Final Four isn't promised to anybody," Krzyzewski said. "But for a while there, it seemed like it was promised to us. For about nine years, it seemed like it was."

———————

Nothing was promised to Krzyzewski when he was hired in 1981 after five seasons at Army. Although Duke had won twenty games in each of the three previous seasons, the talent level had thinned, and a rebuilding job faced whoever was coming in to replace Bill Foster, the coach who never seemed to embrace the unique situation a coach has at Duke, and therefore, left the Blue Devils for the opportunity to coach at South Carolina.

And although he had taken a moribund Army program

and breathed life into it, guiding it to consecutive National Invitation Tournament appearances, Krzyzewski was hardly a household name in ACC country. And the few households that did know his name, certainly couldn't pronounce it. When the Blue Devils announced the hiring of Krzyzewski after the 1980 season, the headline in the Duke student paper actually read: THIS IS NOT A TYPO.

Three years later, Blue Devils fans were begging for Krzyzewski's job, and headline writers were looking for epitaphs on his Duke career. The Blue Devils went 48-47 in that time, Krzyzewski's initial forays into recruiting future Blue Devils was a disaster, and the only emotion thicker in the area than the grief of Duke fans was the outright jubilation nine miles down the road at the University of North Carolina, where they hate the Blue Devils every bit as much as they love the Tar Heels. (Truth be told, Duke fans hate the Tar Heels as much as they love their Blue Devils. Call the intensity between the two programs dangerous, obsessive or even downright pathetic, but don't call it one-sided.)

Then Krzyzewski's recruiting changed. And so did the fate of his program, which in turn, affected the balance of power around the country. In 1982, Krzyzewski signed the first of what would be for Duke, over the next seventeen years, three monster recruiting classes. A program lacking in talent suddenly had as much of it as anyone, and if it seemed like the change happened overnight – well, it did. Krzyzewski brought in Johnny Dawkins, Mark Alarie, David Henderson and Jay Bilas, who, over the next four years, would score a combined 7,323 points. By their senior season, in 1986, Duke had been to three consecutive NCAA tournaments, and reached its first Final Four under Krzyzewski.

In the years after the Dawkins-Alarie-Henderson-Bilas coup, Krzyzewski and Duke added more recruits who ensured the 1986 season was no one-year wonder. Tommy Amaker had signed in 1983, followed by Billy King and

Kevin Strickland in 1984. Danny Ferry was a landmark addition in 1985, because as Krzyzewski pointed out, Ferry was the first player avidly recruited by North Carolina who turned down the renowned Dean Smith and the Tar Heels for the callow Krzyzewski and Blue Devils. There would be more. Smith desperately wanted Grant Hill in 1994, but Hill chose Duke. So did an angry power forward, Christian Laettner, in 1992, and a fiery, sullen point guard, Bobby Hurley, in 1993.

After the breakthrough in 1986, there would be more Final Fours. More expectations. More time demands. Once upon a time, Krzyzewski answered the phone in his office. He almost never turned down an interview request. By 1999, not only had Krzyzewski long since stopped answering his phone, he also granted almost no interview requests, and once went so far as to conduct a conference call with the local media, bringing writers from all over the state into Cameron Indoor Stadium, then chatting with them over a speaker phone – while he sat roughly twenty feet away, down the hall, unseen by anyone, signing autographs for fans who had requested them by mail. That bit of media manipulation was a front-page story the next day in the Raleigh newspaper.

That was 1999. But a few years back, Krzyzewski didn't seem to know how to say no, and if he did know, he certainly wouldn't bring himself to do it. As the Final Four appearances mounted, so did the speaking engagements, the coaching clinics, the autograph sessions. Mixed in there were a pair of national championships, the first in 1991, then another the very next season.

After the second NCAA title, Krzyzewski spent the summer with the 1992 U.S. Olympic basketball team, the original "Dream Team" of Michael Jordan, Magic Johnson, Larry Bird, Charles Barkley, Patrick Ewing and other top basketball players. Two years later, Duke reached the 1994 Final Four, the seventh in that glorious nine-year stretch, a stretch that seemed like it would last forever.

It lasted only twelve more games. That's how far into the 1994-95 season Krzyzewski lasted before he gave out. Technically he was diagnosed as suffering from exhaustion, but fitting what Krzyzewski had been through, over the past several years, into one nice little word was just a bit of cosmetics to give the headline writers something to put at the top of the page.

KRZYZEWSKI OUT;

CITES EXHAUSTION

See how it fits in a double-decker headline? Quite nicely. But it doesn't fit what really happened, why the dream coach of the dream college basketball program would crumble to pieces at the height of his career. No, it wasn't as simple as exhaustion.

There was depression. Eighteen months earlier, one of his best friends had died. Jimmy Valvano, the glowing, charming, hyper coach for years at N.C. State, was diagnosed with terminal cancer in 1992, and died April 28, 1993. Between diagnosis and death, Valvano and Krzyzewski forged a friendship they hadn't enjoyed while coaching against one another. The death of Valvano, just one year older, shook Krzyzewski like nothing since his father had died of a heart attack in 1969.

There was confusion. Krzyzewski had lost his close relationship with his good friend and mentor, Indiana coach Bobby Knight, who seemingly couldn't handle the success of his protege. Knight, who more than anyone else is responsible for Krzyzewski getting into coaching, and who also helped him get his jobs at Army and Duke, blew off Krzyzewski twice when his Indiana teams played Duke in the 1990s. The first blowoff left Krzyzewski hurt, questioning. The second left him numb.

There was agony. Shortly after practice began in that 1994-95 season, Krzyzewski had undergone surgery on a herniated disc that had left his left leg weak and his back in chronic pain. Impatient to get back to his inexperienced, rudderless team, Krzyzewski returned much too soon, and twelve games into the season, his mistake nearly cost him his career. Forced to give up coaching for the rest of the season, Krzyzewski watched as his dynasty crumbled. The Blue Devils went 4-15 the rest of the way, and his reaction was to offer his resignation to Duke Athletic Director Tom Butters. Butters refused to accept Krzyzewski's offer, but that did little to ease the coach's suffering.

"The toughest thing was when the team lost, because it made me feel guilty," he told *Sports Illustrated* later that year. "It was like an out-of-body experience, like one of those movies where you can pull back and look at yourself, like *A Christmas Carol*. And you say, I can't believe I'm doing all these outside things that have nothing to do with coaching. I mean, how could you do all those things ... It's impossible."

———————

Krzyzewski returned the following season, tuned out as many distractions as possible, and the next year signed his second monster recruiting class. The cupboard wasn't as bare as it had been when he took the Duke job after the 1980 season, but it was at its lowest point since then. Krzyzewski remedied that by signing an even better class than the one from 1982, getting four of the top fifteen players in the country: Elton Brand, William Avery, Shane Battier and Chris Burgess.

Their first team, in 1997-98, won thirty-two games, finished the regular season ranked No. 1 in the country and lost by two points in the South regional final to eventual national champion Kentucky – after leading Kentucky by seventeen with less than ten minutes to play.

Their second team, had it scored four more points on March 29, 1999, might have gone down as the best in Duke history. Brand was the National Player of the Year, Avery was one of the country's premier point guards, Battier was a deluxe defender and underappreciated scorer and Burgess was a super sub. The team also included Langdon, an All-American shooting guard, gritty Chris Carrawell and freshman sixth man Corey Maggette, considered by many NBA executives to be the best NBA prospect at Duke – or anywhere else in the United States.

"No matter what happens in the championship game," second-year North Carolina coach Bill Guthridge said the day before Duke played Connecticut, "I think Duke is the best team in the country. It doesn't matter who wins the game, because anything can happen in forty minutes, but there's no question Duke has the best team in the country."

Guthridge, Smith's assistant for thirty years and a member of the Tar Heels staff when they won national titles in 1982 and 1993, called the 1998-99 Blue Devils more dominant even than either of North Carolina's NCAA champions, even the 1982 squad that had Michael Jordan, James Worthy and Sam Perkins. "I can't remember a year when the No. 1 team was so clearly better than everyone else in the country like Duke was this year," Guthridge said.

Five years after the 13-18 meltdown of 1994-95, Duke was incredibly healthy, but Krzyzewski still was hurting. The pain from his back problems of several years ago had seeped into his left hip, and the pain was obvious. At the 1999 Final Four, NCAA officials used golf carts to whisk players and coaches from their locker rooms to the interview areas. With Connecticut's Jim Calhoun, Michigan State's Tom Izzo and Ohio State's Jim O'Brien, the golf cart was a courtesy. With Krzyzewski, it was an absolute necessity.

"We know Coach is hurting, but he never says anything to us about it," said Avery, the sophomore point guard. "I don't think he'd tell us if his hip was falling off.

It's just something everyone already knows."

By the weekend of the Final Four, the hip replacement surgery a week away, Krzyzewski was walking gingerly, as if the bottoms of his shoes were lined with egg shells. He spent most of his practices coaching from a chair at courtside, choosing to let assistants Quin Snyder, Johnny Dawkins and David Henderson handle most of the hands-on instruction.

Before games throughout the season, Krzyzewski had slowly walked from the locker room to the Duke bench, where he eased himself down into his chair, occasionally blowing out a puff of breath from the exertion of it all. During the pregame player introductions, Krzyzewski lowered himself farther, dropping to a knee in front of his five starters and bumping fists with each one as their names were announced to the crowd. Sometimes, between fist-bumps, Krzyzewski wiped the sweat from his brow. He was hurting.

The procedure was front-page news in Durham and Raleigh, and *The News & Observer* went so far as to run a four-color chart of what Krzyzewski's old hip must have looked like – lines pointed out "rough bone," "bone spurs" and "worn cartilage" – and how his new hip would appear. Hospital officials termed the procedure a success, and again reminded fans and well-wishers to get daily updates on Krzyzewski's rehabilitation through the Internet. One such update read: "4/7/99 4:00 p.m. – Coach Krzyzewski remains in good condition. For more information, check out THE LATEST."

A click to THE LATEST revealed two interesting hip-related tidbits. The first was a biography on the surgeon who performed the procedure, Dr. Thomas Parker Vail. The second was a background feature on the history of the procedure itself. Who knew, for example, that there has been better than a ninety percent success rate on all the hip replacement surgeries performed since the British surgeon Sir John Charnley first crafted an artificial hip out of plastic?

Krzyzewski went into the operating room in a good mood. About thirty-six hours before rolling into the operating room, Krzyzewski had taken a phone call from a young man in Juneau, Alaska, named Carlos Boozer, a 6-foot-9, 245-pound power forward rated among the top ten high school seniors in the country. Boozer wanted to let Krzyzewski know he would be coming to Duke to play basketball for the Blue Devils. Boozer became the fifth player from the high school class of 1999 to sign with Duke, joining three other schoolboy All-Americans in a recruiting class some analysts said was better even than Duke's hauls from 1997 (Brand, Avery, etc.) and 1982 (Alarie, Dawkins, etc.).

"It's a good time," said noted recruiting analyst Bob Gibbons of Lenoir, North Carolina, "to be Mike Krzyzewski."

And a great time to be on the outside watching the peculiar dance that is the Duke-North Carolina rivalry. Not even the real-life intrusion of major surgery could pierce the fantasy that is Duke basketball and the emotions it stirred within fans of both programs, as well as the media. The day Krzyzewski underwent surgery, a Durham television station led its nightly news program with nearly two full minutes of coverage of the "developing situation." Among the stories that weren't deemed as important to the television station's viewing audience as Krzyzewski's new hip were the murder charges brought against 11-year-old Durham-area twin boys in the shooting death of their father; the violent death of a local law enforcement officer; and the looming specter of an unidentified sexual predator prowling area parks.

As the newscast began, cameras rolled as Dr. Thomas P. Vail said the two-hour surgery "went really well from the beginning." Coverage then shifted to Krzyzewski's wife, Mickie, who promised that her husband, and therefore the rest of the Duke program, would be "even meaner" in 1999-2000.

A web site not officially affiliated with the University of North Carolina, but which employs the radio commentators for UNC football and basketball games, poked fun of the excessive coverage of Krzyzewski's surgery. A similar web site run by Duke fans, albeit not connected in any way to the Blue Devils' broadcast teams, lashed back at what it called the "callous" North Carolina fan site exacting a form of revenge by parodying North Carolina's shocking first-round loss a month earlier in the NCAA Tournament to underdog Weber State in Seattle by relating this joke: "What's the quickest way from Seattle to Chapel Hill? Ride with the North Carolina basketball team."

Mercifully, Mike Krzyzewski himself wasn't shown on the newscasts the night of his surgery. Doctors said he was healing quite nicely, and looking forward to taking his first steps with his new hip later in the week.

Film at 11.

———

Chapter Two

A COLUMBO IN A STRANGE NEW WORLD

The playground has disappeared, basically. Two metal backboards sway in the wind, but kids no longer play basketball here. The rims fell off the backboards years ago, or were torn off, and were never replaced. The backboards may not have their rims any more, but they are the survivors nonetheless. Several feet away is a single pole jutting about twelve feet into the Chicago air, its backboard missing.

The asphalt is sun-bleached and cracked, grass poking out in a bold, if pathetic, struggle for life. A sign posted nearby says, "Ball Playing Allowed," but this is merely wishful thinking. Nobody plays ball here anymore. This is the old playground of Christopher Columbus Public School on the north side of Chicago.

Years ago, the park was overrun by a local gang that called itself "The Columbos." One Columbo went on to become a loan officer. Another became a business comptroller. A third became a basketball coach at Duke.

This playground, this memory of better times, is where Mike Krzyzewski learned the game of basketball.

He wasn't Mike back then, though. Friends called him Mickey, and he called his friends "Columbos." They were a gang, but not the kind of gang you see nowadays roaming the streets of Chicago. They were a 1950s gang, the urban Andy Griffith kind of gang that got high on basketball, baseball and pinochle, arguing about the White Sox and the Cubs, laughing at very little on the stoops outside their two-story walk-ups.

Krzyzewski was Mickey, and his friends were Moe and Porky, Twams and Sell, Glos and Dicker. And what they had, well, it was good.

"It was never bad, being together with those guys," Krzyzewski said. "It was a sure thing. You didn't have to worry about whatever it is people worry about. You just knew that being together was going to be something excellent. It was a product of how you grew up in Chicago. There was always pride around you. People swept the streets. And they trusted their children."

They talked about everything, the Columbos. They talked about nothing. It was always good for a belly laugh when Steve "Sell" Selsky would break the silence by announcing, "Let's sit around and think about who we don't like."

On the fields of play, the crew-cutted Mickey Krzyzewski was the leader of the Columbos. In baseball he was the center fielder, and when he dreamed, he dreamed that he was a center fielder in the major leagues. Mickey Mantle had the right name, but Krzyzewski was never Mantle. He was "Vada" – for Vada Pinson, a hardworking but much less gifted center fielder than Mantle. Krzyzewski also was the bucket-filling point guard, maybe not the best athlete in the group – OK, he definitely wasn't the best athlete in the group – but he was the best basketball player, the best leader.

It was Mickey Krzyzewski, in fact, who organized basketball games for his middle school team at St. Helen's. The players first asked the nuns at St. Helen's to get them into the Catholic League, but when the nuns showed no interest in such a secular pursuit, Krzyzewski went out and got his team into the league himself. Then he scheduled games, and made sure everyone on both teams knew about them in advance.

"He always wanted to get the game started, to do something," said Larry Kusch, known among the Columbos as "Twams." "A bunch of us liked to sit on the stairs and talk about what we were going to do. Mike didn't do as much sitting as the rest of us. He was a natural born leader; he was a leader back then. He had that magic. Just something about that guy. He was usually out there getting things accomplished."

That's how Emily and Bill Krzyzewski raised their boys. They didn't tolerate any foolishness. Mike's brother, Bill, older by five years, became a captain in the Chicago Fire Department.

"The way we grew up, you always had to go on to the next thing," Krzyzewski said. "You made a good loaf of bread? Well, here's another to make. My brother has to fill an eclair at 5 o'clock in the morning? Well, there's two dozen more to fill by 5:30. It's a way of keeping your feet on the ground, and that's embedded in me."

So, too, is winning. According to his friends, Krzyzewski was the Columbo most likely to have happy teammates.

"You wanted to be on his team because you knew he would win," said Dennis Mlinski, who answered to "Moe" around the Columbos. "He knew how to get you to play better, even in high school. You wanted to be on his side because of his confidence. He didn't scream for the spotlight, and he made you play better. I look back now and see his ability to be a leader even then. He's got a special gift."

And not a bad right jab. Although the Columbos called themselves a gang, they weren't into violence. "A gang to us was five guys and a basketball hoop," Kusch said.

Sometimes, however, a little violence became necessary. Every now and then the Columbos would buck up against another gang at the local recreation center, both sides wanting control of the basketball court or the radio dial or whatever. When that happened, the recreation director always settled it the same way: Each gang was to pick one member from its group, and those two boys would settle it in the boxing ring. Gloves were worn, of course.

Mickey usually won the fight. Of course.

Krzyzewski was left to his own devices as a boy because both parents worked. People wonder how it is, decades later at Duke, that Krzyzewski could work himself to the point of exhaustion. He learned about hard work from his parents. Bill and Emily Krzyzewski were first-generation immigrants from Poland. They settled in the north side of Chicago, where Bill shortened his impossible-to-spell last name to "Kross" when he started looking for a job. He found one in downtown Chicago as an elevator operator in Willoughby Tower, where he ushered the city's upper crust to and from work, up and down, up and down, for years. Emily scrubbed floors at the Chicago Athletic Club, and together, she and her husband made enough to afford the upstairs half of a brick two-flat on Cortez Street, a predominantly Polish-American neighborhood in Chicago. Mike shared a room with his older brother, Bill Jr.

Decades after first meeting in their Chicago neighborhood, the Columbos would meet again. It happened during the 1993 NCAA tournament. Coming off back-to-back NCAA championships, Duke opened its quest for title No. 3 at the Rosemont Horizon in Chicago, where the Blue Devils played Southern Illinois just a few miles down the freeway from where the Columbos used to roam the playground at Christopher Columbus Public School.

"All the Columbos (went)," said "Moe" Mlinski. "Everybody was wheeling and dealing for tickets."

The Columbo reunion at Rosemont Horizon left Krzyzewski misty-eyed. "It's as good as anything that has happened to me," he said that week, "especially in these last few years (at Duke). I believe that my buddies and my family in Chicago shared these things with me. I know that. I absolutely know that. They couldn't give me anything better than the knowledge that they did that."

By his sophomore year at Weber High School in Chicago, Krzyzewski was a basketball player without a starting spot on the varsity basketball team. "That killed him," said "Twams" Kusch. "I don't think he was the best athlete in the neighborhood, but he was the most focused. And he focused himself on starting for the basketball team."

One problem. Krzyzewski reported for tryouts the following year with a broken wrist. Still he tried out for Coach Al Ostrowski's team, and he made it, broken bone and all. The next two seasons, Krzyzewski led the Chicago Catholic League in scoring. He was a celebrity in his neighborhood, where high school sports weren't seen as a means to a college scholarship, but simply as an end by themselves.

"When Mickey was playing his junior and senior years, it was the big social thing to follow him around to games and to go for pizza after," "Twams" Kusch said. "He was a star. Thirty points a game in the Catholic League, and that was a tough league."

The Weber High student newspaper called Krzyzewski the best basketball player in school history, and "Poetry in motion;" a writer for the paper called him, "smooth as silk, elusive eel, dead-eye fancy dribbler."

Ostrowski didn't dabble with such niceties. After one game during Krzyzewski's junior season, when he didn't shoot enough times in a Catholic League loss, Ostrowski stalked over to Krzyzewski in the locker room and threatened him with extra laps every day in practice if he didn't shoot at least twenty-five times a game from then on. Krzyzewski was dumbfounded. It wasn't the sort of support for his basketball game he got at home, where he knew his father loved him dearly and was proud of his basketball talents, even if his father was more the type to tell everyone else – but Mickey – how he felt.

"He talked about me a lot," Krzyzewski has said of his father, "but hardly ever to me. I knew my dad loved me. He just let me have my freedom.

"(Ostrowski) wasn't a great 'X-and-O' guy, but nobody believed in me more than him. He was the first to say to me, 'You're so damned good.'"

But naturally gifted? No. "It was all through hard work," said Rick "Dicker" Glosniak, another of the Columbos. "That really impressed me, that a guy could improve that much, that fast."

———

The summer between his sophomore and junior years of high school changed Krzyzewski's fate forever. It made possible the night during his senior season when he earned the respect of one rival basketball coach, who then set in motion the series of dominoes that fell one by one, taking a former gym rat from Chicago who called himself a Columbo and never dreamed of leaving the neighborhood, and leading that second-generation Polish immigrant to big-time college basketball.

But we're getting ahead of ourselves. In the winter of 1965, in a single game, Weber High against Loyola Academy. Weber point guard Mickey Krzyzewski made his coach happy and squeezed off the mandatory twenty-five shots from the floor, and the result was a thirty-three point bombardment against Loyola. The coach at Loyola, Gene Sullivan, was quoted in local newspapers as saying, "I've seen enough of (Krzyzewski) to last me the rest of my life."

But Sullivan held no grudges. No, instead he did

Krzyzewski perhaps the biggest favor of the Columbo's life. Sullivan called an old friend, who happened to be the head basketball coach at the United States Military Academy, an institution known in the sports pages as, simply, Army. The coach back then at Army is also known in the sports pages.

Bobby Knight.

Knight, now the coach at Indiana, had never seen Krzyzewski play in person. He has said numerous times he had no intentions of recruiting Krzyzewski, even though Krzyzewski did have the extracurricular resume the Army looks for in prospective students. During his final year at Weber High, his classmates voted Krzyzewski senior class president. Knight didn't know anything about that, and he probably wouldn't have cared if he did. Could the little Polish kid play basketball? Was he willing to work? Was he smart? Tough?

Yes, Sullivan told Knight. Yes, yes, yes, yes.

From his office in West Point, New York, Knight began keeping tabs on Krzyzewski's games at Weber High. Sure enough, Knight saw, the kid could play. He shot a little too much – more than a little too much, really – in Knight's opinion, but that could be fixed. That would be fixed. Knight wasn't worried about that.

Knight showed up one night at Bill and Emily's two-flat on the north side of Chicago, hoping to seal the deal on their son, Mickey. Knight was offering a scholarship to Army. Bill and Emily couldn't get over it. A free education? A sure-thing job in the military waiting after graduation? Basketball could do this? They were thrilled.

Mickey was nervous. Leave the neighborhood? Leave the Columbos? In his neighborhood, college certainly was an option – a college you could get to on foot, that is.

"You could go to college," Krzyzewski said years later. "But you couldn't go away to college. My parents really wanted me to go. I wasn't that keen on going. They told me I shouldn't pass up on such a great opportunity. Our family didn't have that many opportunities, so I followed their advice."

Not that it was that simple. Krzyzewski's parents pushed as their son hesitated to jump at what they saw as a gift-wrapped chance to leave the neighborhood and perhaps one day be the kind of man who worked at Willoughby Tower, where Bill operated the elevator, or who worked out at the Chicago Athletic Club, where Emily cleaned the place. One night, according to an article published years later in *Sports Illustrated*, Mom and Dad Krzyzewski had this conversation in the kitchen, knowing full well that their son, in the next room, was listening to every word.

Bill: "I can't believe he's not taking this opportunity. Can you believe he's not taking this opportunity?"

Emily: "If only we'd had such an opportunity."

Bill: "How can he be so dumb as to pass up this opportunity?"

Ultimately Mickey didn't pass up the opportunity. For that, for a full year, he was sorry. Unable to compete in basketball games as a freshman because of NCAA eligibility rules at the time, Krzyzewski found himself competing, instead, against other U.S. Military Academy students in survival courses.

Krzyzewski found himself, for the first time in his life, losing. And losing badly. There was the overnight trip during his freshman year when Krzyzewski, who had lived in the shadow of downtown Chicago his entire life, was asked to pitch a tent along with the rest of the class. While most of the others were nature-savvy enough to dig trenches around their tents in the event of rain in the middle of the night, Krzyzewski simply pitched his tent and went to bed. That night it rained, and he realized his grade for the trip wouldn't be so good when his tent nearly floated away.

That same year Krzyzewski, the two-time Catholic League scoring champion from Chicago, flunked freshman physical education. The problem? It seems Krzyzewski had never learned to swim. "I was a city kid," he explained. "At West Point, I learned how to grow from having my ego hurt."

Speaking of having your ego hurt ... Krzyzewski began learning basketball and life from Bobby Knight, who already had come to certain conclusions about his new point guard.

"I was quick to see Mike could play on our team, but none of it related to what he did in high school," Knight said. "We had better shooters than him. But in becoming the kind of player we wanted him to be, Mike gained an appreciation for basketball that a scorer never could."

In other words, Krzyzewski was made to appreciate the impact of a gritty defense on a game, and the democratic beauty of the pass. Those were his two duties on Knight's basketball team: defense and playmaking. Scoring wasn't one. Shooting? Absolutely not.

On one occasion, Knight told Krzyzewski to go ahead and shoot if he wanted – as long as he didn't complain if Knight broke his arm when he returned to the bench. That message was delivered in the locker room from Knight to Krzyzewski before Army played South Carolina in the 1969 National Invitation Tournament, Krzyzewski's senior year and his second season as Knight's starting point guard. One of the players guarding Krzyzewski that night was a South Carolina guard with a shock of blond hair and a name that Krzyzewski and the rest of the Atlantic Coast Conference basketball world would come to know intimately decades later: Bobby Cremins, the future coach at Georgia Tech.

Meanwhile, during the game, Krzyzewski found himself alone with the basketball on the wing. If this were a Catholic League game under Coach Ostrowski, the ball would have been launched without a second thought. But this wasn't a Catholic League game.

And that wasn't Ostrowski on the sideline.

"I went up and set my hands to shoot," Krzyzewski said, "and then, 'Boom!' I pass."

Said Knight: "Most kids say, 'Here I am, play me.' We told Mike he would have to play defense and handle the ball. Obviously, Mike listened, because he ended up playing."

He played even when he probably shouldn't have. During a tournament at Kentucky over the Christmas holidays, Krzyzewski absorbed a frightful blow to his upper head against Bradley and left the game with fuzzy vision and severe hemorrhaging in one eye. Krzyzewski returned to the game later, and was standing at the foul line with two shots to win – or lose. Krzyzewski made both, and Army won.

All that did was set up one of the more emotionally painful nights of Krzyzewski's college career. The Bradley game was a semifinal in the tournament. In the championship game against Kentucky, the host team, the powerhouse Wildcats, led by Dan Issel, wiped out Army. Knight showed no joy over winning the consolation trophy. In the Army locker room after the game, Knight spat on the runner-up trophy and dented a locker with his foot. Army went on to lose its next three games, and Krzyzewski, the captain, took the losses as hard inwardly as Knight seemed to be taking them outwardly.

"It was the toughest period of my life as a player," Krzyzewski said. "I didn't understand what was happening, and I felt responsible for what was happening."

Knight never took aside his fiery point guard and explained the losing streak. He never told Krzyzewski whether or not it was his fault. He left Krzyzewski to guess, to fill in the blanks, and Krzyzewski filled them in a manner that left him with a gnawing pain inside. It wouldn't be the last time Knight would disappoint Krzyzewski, though Knight did come through for his player later that year.

On March 1, 1969, Knight awarded Krzyzewski with a game ball for his play in a victory against arch-rival, Navy. Still in the locker room, reveling in the victory, Krzyzewski received a phone call from a family member in Chicago. His father had suffered a massive cerebral hemorrhage. Krzyzewski immediately began throwing his things together to return home, and was surprised to see Knight also in a frenzy, getting his things together as well. "I'm going with you," Knight said.

They arrived in Chicago hours later, but it was too late. Bill Krzyzewski was dead.

After finishing his playing career at Army, which he capped by making second-team All-NIT as a senior, Krzyzewski went on to play for the All-Armed Forces team, where he ran into another coach who would make an impact on his future coaching style. Whereas Knight was restrictive and conservative, controlling the pace of the game from his seat on the bench, All-Armed Forces coach Hal Fisher allowed his players more freedom, presenting them with choices and allowing them to make decisions on their own.

"He treated you like men," Krzyzewski said of Fisher. "He gave me an opportunity to express my ideas. He wanted to hear what I had to say. He let me be more of a coach than a player."

Two coaches, two completely different coaching styles. Krzyzewski became a disciple of both, but a copycat of neither. From Knight he picked up much of his big-picture technique – the emphasis on man-to-man defense starting from the half-court line; the unpredictable motion offense that required intelligent players to make the correct reads; the down-to-the-last-minute structure of practices and game days. From Fisher, Krzyzewski pulled some of the more subtle points of coaching – giving his players freedom to succeed and fail, and how to turn both situations into learning devices; finding a point guard who would become an extension of Krzyzewski on the court; remembering that the game is, above all else, a game.

When it came to communication with his players, Krzyzewski seemed to have learned his biggest lesson not from a basketball coach, but a geometry teacher at Weber High School. His name was Francis Rog, and he was a Catholic priest. Rog got Krzyzewski to open up, on topics like life and religion, like no one had before.

"Growing up, I was basically a person who kept everything within me," Krzyzewski said. "The only way I would bring it out would be in a moment when I was not guarded. I could talk to somebody I could trust."

That somebody was Father Rog. Krzyzewski saw him one day sitting in a chair after basketball practice outside the Weber High varsity locker room. Krzyzewski began talking to Rog that day about faith. In the process, he learned a lesson he would take with him to Duke.

"He was always there for me, always around," Krzyzewski said. "The lesson from that is someone can be an easy guy to talk to – but it's not easy for you to talk to the easy guy to talk to, if he's always in his office."

Ostrowski taught him to fill his players with confidence. Knight taught him basic basketball principles. Fisher taught him to let go as a coach. Rog taught him how to be there, how to listen.

Krzyzewski has tried to put it all together.

"What I'm striving for is utopia," Krzyzewski said. "I try to find some way to integrate everybody, allow them all to improve and have them understand their places."

———

His name was Mickey. Her name was Mickie.

They met in 1967, Mike "Mickey" Krzyzewski and Mickie Marsh. He was a basketball player. She was a stewardess. Their first date was a Martha and the Vandellas concert in Chicago.

Krzyzewski was intimidated, so he fibbed a bit. He told Mickie she was one of three girls he had considered asking to the concert, which apparently was the truth. However, he was unsure how she would react – unsure how anyone would react in the late 1960s, with the United States' largely unpopular involvement in the Vietnam War – to the news that he was at Army. So, he also told her he was a student at a trade school in the North. Soon after, he told her the truth.

They were married in the summer of 1969 at the Catholic Chapel at West Point, barely four hours after Krzyzewski had received his diploma.

Three years later, Krzyzewski was a commissioned officer in the U.S. Army. He found himself in the northernmost part of South Korea, hard by the demilitarized zone. Krzyzewski was the commanding officer of an Army recreational compound. This wasn't exactly Saigon, but it wasn't Club Med, either.

Krzyzewski was unbearably unhappy. About a year after they were married, he and Mickie had a daughter, Debbie. While Krzyzewski was in South Korea, Mickie and Debbie were back in Alexandria, Virginia, living with Mickie's parents.

"I felt cut off from everything I cared about," Krzyzewski said. "You had nothing going for you – nothing. I felt so lonely."

The feeling was mutual back in Alexandria.

"I was worried about him and he was worried about me," Mickie Krzyzewski told *The Charlotte Observer* in 1991. "But, most of all, I was worried about us."

In their loneliness the Krzyzewskis resorted to drastic measures. Back in Alexandria, Mickie packed her bags, grabbed Debbie's diapers and bought a plane ticket to Seoul. Romantic? No question. Wise? Probably not.

The only way to be together was to break compound rules, and that's just what the Krzyzewski family did. Wives and children were not allowed on the compound, but Mickie and Debbie lived there anyway. Mother and daughter hid out in a supply room for three months, sometimes ducking behind ladders and storage bins to protect their cover.

Their bed was a cot. Their oven and stove was a single hot plate. Their rest room was a public facility in an Army movie theater, which Mickie and Debbie grew accustomed to sneaking into and hurrying out, undetected. Taking a hot shower was even trickier, but Mickie and Mike found a way. While her husband stood guard, Mickie and Debbie hustled into the Army shower every night at 8 p.m.

This is how the Krzyzewski family lived for months.

Late one night, the Krzyzewskis were huddled in the supply room when the sound of exploding gunfire erupted all around them. "I was terrified," Mickie said.

It was only a drill, but the anxious episode raised a question that Mickie had to ask her husband.

"What would we do," she asked, "if this was war?"

Krzyzewski held his wife and said, "I'd get all my men together and we'd throw basketballs and popcorn at them."

Looking back, Mickie Krzyzewski wonders at the sanity of those months in South Korea.

"It was all such a crazy, crazy time," she said. "I don't know if it was love, dependency or what, but we needed to be there together, no matter the circumstances."

———

The Army scholarship Knight offered Krzyzewski provided a free education and free basketball, but it came with a price: a five-year obligation in the U.S. Army. Krzyzewski spent those five years, even that time in South Korea, coaching basketball, positioning himself for his first job in college. His first coaching job was running Army base teams abroad. From there, he moved on to the U.S. Military Academy Prep School in Belvoir, Virginia, an ideal situation in that he was able to coach for two years

Once close friends, Coach K and Indiana's Bobby Knight, shown here in the late 1960s when Krzyzewski was Knight's point guard at Army, drifted apart after Krzyzewski's Duke team surpassed Knight's Hoosiers.

while Mickie was able to return to her home state.

By 1974, Krzyzewski had risen to the rank of Captain, his military future stretching ahead like a red carpet. At the same time, he had essentially risen as far as he could as a basketball coach in the U.S. Military Academy. It was time to make a career choice.

Bobby Knight, his former coach at Army, made the choice easy for him. By then Knight had left Army for Indiana, and in 1974 he had an opening on his staff for a graduate-assistant coach. He thought of Krzyzewski, and called his former point guard with a job offer. Krzyzewski accepted, resigning his U.S. Army commission and secure, if predictable, future to become the low man on a most unpredictable totem pole: college basketball coach.

Krzyzewski spent that year with Knight at Indiana honing his knowledge of the motion offense and constantly switching, communicating man-to-man defense. Most of all, Krzyzewski was adding to his resumé, making himself more marketable for the time he hoped would come, when a college would consider him to be a head basketball coach himself.

It came sooner than he expected. And from a place he might never have guessed.

During that same 1974 season that Krzyzewski was an Indiana graduate assistant, the Army basketball team continued its slide without Knight. That season, Army hit rock bottom: 3-22. The coaching position at Army opened up, and Knight, who, at Indiana, already was running one of the more powerful programs in the country, exerted some of his famous influence. Knight made a few phone calls to some of his old friends at Army, and soon Krzyzewski was back at West Point, New York, interviewing for the vacant head coaching position.

It didn't take long for members of the Army selection committee to wonder aloud why West Point should hire someone who, as Krzyzewski had done one year earlier, resigned his commission as a captain. Craftily, Krzyzewski turned that decision around and put it in his favor, telling the selection committee the resignation of his commission merely showed how badly he wanted to become a college basketball coach. And now, Krzyzewski was telling the selection committee, he wanted to use what the Army had taught him to rebuild its basketball program.

One hundred and twenty people applied for the job. It was offered only to Krzyzewski. He was 28, and he was a head coach at the NCAA Division I level. He was the head coach of his alma mater. He had never been so much as a full-time assistant coach at the college level, and now he was running his own program.

"It was scary," he said, "but it was incredibly exciting and liberating."

He was young and relatively inexperienced, but in many ways Krzyzewski was the perfect fit for Army. He went into the job with no false illusions of being able to recruit the top high school players in the country. He went in knowing a successful season was winning more games than losing, period, and that a run deep into the NCAA tournament every March would be asking too much. He went into it realistic, understanding that the military believes the best way to teach a young soldier to win is by introducing failure. Learn how to fail, the theory goes, and eventually you learn how to win in the face of failure. That's what the job at Army called for. And that's what Krzyzewski brought.

He also brought Bobby Knight-type basketball, and soon found Bobby Knight-type success. Motion offense, sticky man-to-man defense. Players diving for loose balls. Hard fouls – clean, but hard.

In Krzyzewski's first season, the Cadets went 11-14. Then, the breakthrough. Army won twenty games in 1976-77, and nineteen more in 1977-78. Army, which hadn't been to the National Invitation Tournament since Knight coached and Krzyzewski played in 1969, received an invitation to the tournament in 1978. Although lesser seasons followed, a 14-11 mark in 1979 and a 9-17 record in 1980, Krzyzewski had made a name for himself as one of the top young coaches in the country. He had a lot to offer: Division I playing experience under Knight, a year of coaching under Knight, and – although he was only 33 years old – five years as a head coach in Division I, with a 73-59 record to show for it at a school where winning just doesn't come that easily. Although no one could know it at the time, after Army went 14-11 under Krzyzewski in 1979, the Cadets would post just one winning season in the next two decades.

Not that Krzyzewski was going to be there to watch it happen. He had become a hot coaching commodity, and during that 9-17 season in 1980, he received two intriguing phone calls that proved it. The first was from Knight, telling Krzyzewski that he had recommended Iowa State fill its coaching void by hiring Krzyzewski after the season.

The second call came a month later, right after Army had finished its season, from Duke Athletic Director Tom Butters. Duke basketball coach Bill Foster had announced his resignation after the season to become the coach at South Carolina. Butters wanted to talk to Krzyzewski about the opening – in Lexington, Kentucky, where the Blue Devils were to play in the first round of the NCAA tournament. Knowing how ferociously the North Carolina media covered his basketball program, Butters wanted to meet Krzyzewski away from Durham for privacy as much as anything.

Like the Iowa State opportunity, this one had come knocking on Krzyzewski's door because of Knight, who actually had recommended to Butters another former Indiana assistant, Ole Miss head coach Bob Weltlich, for the opening. Butters had learned about Krzyzewski through other avenues of information, but when he asked Knight about the Army coach, Knight was effusive. "He has all my best qualities," Knight said of Krzyzewski, "and none of my bad ones."

Butters let Krzyzewski leave Lexington without a job offer, and that nearly ended Duke's chances at him. When he returned to West Point, Krzyzewski had received a message from Iowa State, offering him the head job there. When asked, Knight counseled Krzyzewski to take it. Krzyzewski thought about it, then called Iowa State to ask for more time. Butters made that move pay off a few days later when he called Krzyzewski and asked him to come to Durham for a second interview.

Again, Butters let Krzyzewski get away without extending a job offer – in a manner of speaking. Krzyzewski was at the Raleigh-Durham Airport, waiting for his flight back to New York, when he heard his name paged. Standing there in the airport with a travel bag in one hand and a plane ticket for home in the other, Krzyzewski found the nearest courtesy phone, and there was Butters on the other end, asking a simple question:

"If I offer you this job," Butters said, "will you take it?"

———

Chapter Three

COACH WHO?

Kenny Dennard was about as far south as he could be, and still be in the United States, when he learned he had a new basketball coach. This was spring break for Dennard, a 6-foot-7 junior forward at Duke. Well, it wasn't officially spring break. That had come and gone, and Dennard had missed it while playing out the season with the Duke basketball team. So this was his spring break, his private, one-man revolt against a system that denied him the chance to soak up sun rays and gulp mixed drinks for a week in March like so many other college students.

Dennard was sitting in the bar at The Pier House on Duvall Street in Key West, Florida, drinking a mai tai. Good drink. Fruity, but strong. The Pier House, located at the bottom tip of Key West, billed itself as the southernmost hotel in the country. Was it? Who knows? It sounded good to Dennard, so there he was when the sports broadcast on the bar television set began talking about the Duke basketball team. Dennard lifted his head from his drink and listened.

"The sportscaster said Duke had named a new coach, and then he stumbled over the name," Dennard said. "People in the bar went, 'Bless you.'"

No they didn't. Dennard was joking about the "bless you" part, but his joke, nearly twenty years after the fact, sums up fairly well the tone of the press conference in 1980 that announced the hiring of the Blue Devils' fourth coach since legendary leader Vic Bubas had retired at the end of the 1969 season.

The hype leading up to that press conference was typical for Atlantic Coast Conference country. Newspapers around the state tried desperately to keep up with Duke Athletic Director Tom Butters, who foiled them by interviewing candidates outside of Durham, in hotel rooms in cities where Duke was playing in the NCAA tournament. The day before the announcement, the local paper in Durham still didn't know who the next coach would be, but the paper felt it had a pretty good idea: either Ole Miss coach Bob Weltlich, Old Dominion coach Paul Webb or Duke assistant coach Bob Wenzel, the holdover from Bill Foster's staff. Foster had resigned after the season to take the job at South Carolina.

Feeling pretty good about the chances of Weltlich, Webb or Wenzel being the next coach, the Durham paper led its story that Tuesday morning with, "Duke's new basketball coach will be chosen in the next two days, and one thing's for sure – his last name will begin with the letter 'W'– as in win."

The next night, a Wednesday, Duke held its press conference to announce the new coach. Butters stepped to the podium and introduced to the ACC basketball world Mike Krzyzewski. Coach K, not Coach W. Butters then had a little joke at the Durham paper's expense. "I know what you're going to do," he said to a Durham writer. "You're going to say you were right, that the new man is Coach Who."

Well, yes. As far as most people who followed Duke

basketball were concerned, Mike Krzyzewski was indeed: Coach Who?

Duke's occasionally clever, always rebellious student paper, *The Chronicle*, bleated, "THIS IS NOT A TYPO" in its headline over the story announcing Krzyzewski as the new coach.

ACC, meet Coach Question Mark.

He was how old? (33) He had how many years experience as a head coach in Division I? (five) He came from where? (Army) His last team at Army had how awful a record? (9-17) It was true that Army's front line averaged 6-foot-4 across the board, helping to account for such a dismal record, but skeptics didn't want to hear excuses. They wanted to hear that Weltlich had been hired after turning Ole Miss into a respectable program, or that Wenzel had been rewarded for his loyalty by being promoted from Foster's assistant to his permanent replacement. The skeptics wanted a name they had heard of.

Krzyzewski wasn't it.

"I realize Mike's not a household name, and I realize that's a difficulty to some people," Butters said that day. "But he will be a household name. There is no doubt in my mind that Mike is the brightest young basketball mind in America. The job was not offered to anyone else. He is my first choice, and he will remain my first choice."

Coach Who?

Standing there in front of a room full of reporters, his eyes, hair and skin dark, his face chiseled as if out of granite, his angular nose the most striking feature on his face, Krzyzewski looked very much like a young Al Pacino in *The Godfather*. Krzyzewski flashed some of the self-deprecating wit that would serve him well in the lean years to follow. "The last name is spelled K-R-Z-Y-Z-E-W-S-K-I, and if you think that's bad, you should have seen what it was before I changed it. I've been called a lot of things, but Mike or Coach K is fine with me. That's what the

Coach K meets the media after being introduced as Duke's
new head coach.

players usually settle for, and that's fine with me."

In another corner of the room, Butters was assuring skeptical sports writers that he had dreamed initially of hiring a big name – and he wasn't talking about Krzyzewski and his ten-letter, three-syllable Scrabble nightmare.

"Damn right, I started out thinking in terms of a big name. If your football coach quits, the first name you think of is Bear Bryant. You do think big names. But the more I assessed what we had, the more I reacquainted myself with my feelings toward the university and this program, and the more convinced I was that a big name was not necessarily all we wanted. We had a long, long list of names, but I wanted to make sure I didn't miss any bright, young coaches during our search.

"I like track records. Mike has one. I don't think this is a gamble. Would it have been any less of a gamble if we'd hired a name coach? If this is gambling, it's where I'd like to put my money. I never thought the decisions I was going to make would get unanimous approval. A man has to search his soul and get the best advice he can."

Butters especially liked the advice of Indiana coach Bobby Knight. "Knight doesn't say much he doesn't mean, and he told me Mike was bright and brilliant – and he meant it. He kept talking about Mike's character. I like a man with high character. When we checked Mike out, everything Knight had said was accurate."

Back in Key West, Dennard was left to wonder about his new coach. Coach Who?

"I didn't know who he was," Dennard said. "No, I had never heard of Mike Krzyzewski, but that didn't really matter as much back then as it would now. This was B.C. – Before Cable. There was no manic sports reporting on a national level like there is today, where you know about every coach at every decent program because of March Madness and all that. Sentimentally, I know Duke fans were wondering about this guy: a Bobby Knight disciple, a

West Point graduate, a really young coach.

"Obviously in hindsight Tom Butters looks like a genius, but at the time it was a risky move."

If Krzyzewski felt pressure to make Butters look like a genius, he didn't show it that first day on the job. He even went so far as to tweak the nose of the state's basketball writers, chiding them for guessing wrong on the identity of the new Duke coach. "I guess you guys haven't been working hard enough," he said.

Then he got serious.

"There are times when you know something is right for you," he said, "and I felt from the beginning of our talks the Duke job is right for me."

Duke fans soon began to disagree.

———————

Krzyzewski hadn't merely been hired as a head basketball coach at a strong Division I program. He had been entrusted with a college basketball tradition with deep roots. College basketball in the state of North Carolina began at Duke in 1906, less than two decades after a Springfield, Massachusetts, physical education teacher named James Naismith invented the game with peach baskets.

In those days shortly after the turn of the twentieth century, Duke wasn't known as Duke, but as Trinity College. A 1900 Trinity College graduate named Wilbur "Cap" Card brought the new game, basketball, to campus, an arrival that was hailed by the student paper, *The Chronicle*: "It is well-nigh a certainty that Trinity is to have another game added to her list of athletic sports in the near future. The game in question is basket ball, one of the most fascinating and most intensely interesting indoor sports known today. Anyone witnessing it will never forget it, the play is extremely fast and vigorous, yet open enough for an onlooker to follow the movement of the ball and the players."

The first basketball game in the state was played March 2, 1906, at Trinity. Wake Forest spoiled things, beating Trinity 24-10, but a legacy had been born. Trinity went 2-3 that season, the scores never reaching the thirties. One game finished 15-5. H.E. Spence, a member of that first Trinity basketball team, explained the low scores in an interview published decades later in the Duke basketball media guide: "It was easy to explain the small scores. First of all, the game was very much slower. The ball was tossed up at the center at the beginning of each quarter as well as the beginning of the game and the half. It was also thrown up after each point scored. Then, too, it was very difficult to throw goals when your guard was tattooing your ribs with his elbows, bumping you with his hip, stepping on your toe, or grabbing you by the belt."

Sounds like a typical Clemson game one hundred years later.

Anyhow, from those beginnings, basketball at Trinity, which would change its name to Duke in the next fifteen years, would take off in 1929 with the arrival of Eddie Cameron, whose name later would adorn the gym on campus. Cameron went 226-99 in fourteen seasons, beginning a streak that continued through the end of the century in which Duke never suffered more than two consecutive losing seasons.

In 1960, Duke hired away a promising assistant from rival N.C. State named Vic Bubas. Like Krzyzewski when he took over at Duke, Bubas was young (31), with no head coaching experience at a big-time powerhouse. Unlike Krzyzewski, Bubas' name already was known throughout the state thanks to his high-profile role on Everett Case's staff at N.C. State, a national heavyweight in the 1950s.

Bubas was known as a recruiting pioneer, inventing some of the techniques coaches use today, targeting high school players early and smothering them with attention from himself and his staff, which included such future big names as Chuck Daly, Hubie Brown and Bucky Waters.

Daly and Brown would go on to coach in the NBA, and Waters would be the head coach down the road at Duke.

"In terms of what a coach is today and what a typical coach was and what a typical program was in 1959, when he took over at Duke, Vic Bubas was more ahead of his time than anyone I've ever seen," former Wake Forest guard and longtime television commentator Billy Packer said in *Four Corners* by Joe Menzer. "If you followed the way he put together a staff, the way he recruited, the organization and all the things that he brought to the table in 1960, and followed that exactly, you would not have been that out of touch in 1998. He was that far ahead of his time in terms of how he would do things for the betterment of his basketball program. I can't think of anybody else in the history of college basketball who has been as far ahead of the times as he was."

One of the first big stars Bubas recruited to Duke was Jay Buckley, who reportedly had an IQ of 160 and who spent one summer at Columbia University on a program funded by NASA.

"Jay," Bubas told Buckley one day, "one of these days I'll be reading about you being the first man on the moon."

"No, coach," Buckley replied, "you'll be there first, looking for ball players."

Bubas found two of the greatest players in Duke history a little closer to home. Art Heyman, a 6-foot-5 forward, signed in 1960 out of New York, and 6-4 Jeff Mullins signed the next year from Kentucky. To get Heyman, an eccentric sort who went on to star in the ABA and drive teammates and coaches crazy with his oddities, Bubas invited the Long Island native to dine at the swanky Manhattan Hotel. Heyman was so impressed, he committed to play for Duke on the spot. To steal Mullins, a native of Lexington, from the hometown of the Kentucky Wildcats, Bubas had to overcome a personal plea from the governor of Kentucky, who all but begged Mullins to play for the Bluegrass State's flagship university.

Together, Heyman and Mullins led Duke to its first Final Four, in 1963. That Duke team was larger than life, mainly because of the tall-tale exploits of Heyman and the bizarre innovations of Bubas. Heyman was so intense, he vomited before every game. He was so strong, he once dislocated Bubas' thumb with a handshake. He was so wild, he once was arrested for transporting a female across state lines for immoral purposes. They registered at a hotel in Myrtle Beach, South Carolina, as Mr. and Mrs. Oscar Robertson in homage to the NBA star whose game Heyman's often was compared to. For his part, Bubas used to have Daly, his assistant, sit in the rafters atop Cameron Indoor Stadium, just so Daly could watch the game from above with binoculars and call down whatever insights he had gleaned to the Duke bench.

By 1966, Duke was challenging the burgeoning dynasty at UCLA. The Blue Devils achieved the No. 1 ranking early that season, won their fourth ACC title in seven years and reached the Final Four before losing to Kentucky.

As it turns out, that was Duke's last hurrah on the national level for a dozen years. Burned out at age 40, Bubas retired after the 1969 season, and the Duke basketball factory listed like a rowboat at sea for the next twelve years. Bill Foster was hired for the 1974-75 season, and after three years of mediocrity, he struck pay dirt. With three veteran stars – center Mike Gminski, forward Gene Banks and guard Jim Spanarkel – leading the way, Duke won twenty-seven games and reached the 1978 national championship game, where the forty-one point heroics of Kentucky's Jack Givens allowed the Wildcats to escape with a 94-88 victory.

Duke was back.

Wasn't it?

In hindsight, Foster didn't do his eventual replacement – Krzyzewski – much of a favor. Two seasons later, after Gminski, the all-time scoring leader in Duke history, and Spanarkel graduated, with Banks, a rising senior,

the only holdover from the glorious Gminski-Banks-
Spanarkel triumvirate, Foster announced he was leaving
to become the coach at South Carolina.

Turns out, Foster left the Duke cupboard all but bare.

Krzyzewski should have known he was in for an uphill
battle when he called a team meeting his first day on the
job, and the two senior players who would become the
leading scorers and captains on his first Duke team
weren't even there. Dennard was still in Key West,
drinking in the sun's rays and who knows what else.
Banks, a 6-foot-7 forward who decided to return to Duke
for his senior season after considering leaving early for
the NBA, compromised – he did leave school, but only for
a week, like the Key West-bound Dennard, after the 1979-
80 season to take his own personal spring break.

"I guess in hindsight it's kind of funny," said Dennard,
who decades later is a businessman in Houston, Texas.
"Coach K had this team meeting, and Gene and I weren't
even there. We'd just left because we thought we needed
a break. But Mike Krzyzewski was not reactionary. He
wasn't mad at us or anything like that. He came in with a
very open mind. I guess he had to know at that point he
was coming into a unique program."

He also was coming into a program on the decline.
Since Banks and Dennard signed in 1976, Foster had failed
to ink any top-flight recruits other than 6'5" guard Vince
Taylor of Lexington, Kentucky, the following year. By the
time Krzyzewski had come to town, Banks and Dennard
were seniors. Taylor was a junior. The sophomore and
freshman classes were weak.

Dennard knows. He was there.

"Not that I can tell what goes on in someone else's
mind, but when Bill Foster decided he was leaving, the
recruiting energies just were not the same for him,"
Dennard said. "That was fairly obvious, in hindsight, even

as it was happening. But I don't want to lay anything on Bill Foster. He came in and built the program back to national prominence.

"I don't know his motives when it came to his recruiting there at the end of his time at Duke. Who knows? It might have been as much for the kids' sake as his own. Maybe he decided he's not going to recruit kids by lying to them that he'll be there for four years, when he knew that wasn't going to be the case. In that sense I admire Coach Foster for not bringing in a bunch of big names and deserting them. That's an admirable quality. But it didn't help the program any."

The level of talent may have been a problem for Krzyzewski coming into his first season at Duke, but confidence wasn't. That's one of the reasons Butters chose the relatively unknown young man from Army in the first place.

"He was very sure of himself, very confident that he would come in with a plan and make it work," Butters said. "I was drawn to that confidence. It wasn't out of control or anything like that. He was someone who seemed aware of his limitations, but also aware of ways of fixing them."

Krzyzewski's self-assurance was flashed for all to see a mere three games into his career at Duke. His third game as coach of the Blue Devils, on December 5, 1980, was against none other than North Carolina. This was Krzyzewski's first look at the Duke-UNC rivalry and, more than that, it was his first encounter with the Tar Heels' legend-in-the-making coach, Dean Smith. North Carolina was ranked No. 10. Duke, though it had won its first two games, was unranked, which it would stay throughout the season. The Tar Heels had three future first-round NBA picks in Al Wood, James Worthy and Sam Perkins, but the Blue Devils hung close before losing 78-76 at Greensboro, North Carolina. Afterward, Krzyzewski was asked how it felt to be coaching against someone of the stature of

Smith. His answer was a hint of things to come, both for Duke and for the Duke-UNC rivalry.

"From a personal standpoint, I enjoy coaching in the best league," Krzyzewski said. "I look forward to that. I wasn't overconfident, but I was confident. I didn't feel anything tonight I haven't felt before. There are a lot of good basketball coaches around, but I have confidence in my ability.

"I'm a good basketball coach, too."

That was the night Krzyzewski got his first up close, personal look at basketball as religion in North Carolina, where four schools within ninety miles of each other – and three within a thirty-minute drive – dominated the landscape, not to mention the sports pages and news broadcasts: Duke in Durham, North Carolina in Chapel Hill, N.C. State in Raleigh and Wake Forest about ninety miles to the west in Winston-Salem. Duke and North Carolina had played that night in something called the Big Four Tournament, a pre-ACC season meeting of the four giants of North Carolina basketball.

There was something else Krzyzewski was quick to learn. Some giants were bigger than others. The University of North Carolina was the state's flagship college, the anchor that produced the most graduates and also drew the support of the majority of the state residents who didn't attend any of the Big Four schools. N.C. State, another public university, was next in line in terms of producing graduates and attracting fans. Behind them were the two small, private schools, Duke and Wake Forest. Krzyzewski thought he was ready for the intensity, the emotion of the Big Four. He thought wrong.

"There's no way you can be prepared for it," he said. "You've got to experience it to begin to understand it. You can never be ready for it completely and the fact is that in this area, you're always going to be a minority. There are going to be many more North Carolina fans. Then there will be more N.C. State fans. Duke and Wake Forest are in a minority."

Krzyzewski no doubt would have been depressed had he known this, but that first Duke team would be his best for three years. The Blue Devils went 17-13 in 1980-81, including a 6-8 mark in the ACC. Nonetheless, Dennard looked back on the season, which fell far short of the glory of 1978, when he was a freshman, with pride.

"Krzyzewski didn't have to do a lot of baby-sitting of us because me and Gene Banks and Vince Taylor (now a junior) had been around the block. I thought we had a great year together, given what we had for talent," Dennard said. "Our record in the conference was pretty admirable compared to what we could have been. We had no center. Mike Gminski was gone. We were playing against guys like (7-foot-4 Virginia All-American center Ralph) Sampson, Worthy, Perkins. We did as well as we could, I'm sure of that."

But it wasn't good enough. Certainly not, when there was North Carolina winning the 1982 national championship less than ten miles away. And certainly not, when there was N.C. State, playing in its third season under a spunky Italian coach named Jim Valvano, winning the national championship the very next year, in 1983. The Wolfpack stunned Houston and the rest of the college basketball world by winning the national championship on Lorenzo Charles' last-second offensive-rebound basket. Valvano and Krzyzewski had been hired in the same year. Krzyzewski's Duke team went 11-17.

Krzyzewski's confidence in his system did little to win him friends among the Duke faithful. He stubbornly refused to play anything but the man-to-man defense he had learned from Knight and implemented at Army, even though the talent gap between his teams, and much of the rest of the ACC, often left his man-to-man defenses helpless. Duke had no answer for Virginia's Sampson or North Carolina's Perkins and Worthy inside, or even gifted wing players like Maryland's Albert King or N.C. State's

Hawkeye Whitney.

Chuck Swenson, an assistant with Krzyzewski at Army and also on his first few teams at Duke, remembers the shock of seeing players like Sampson, Whitney and Perkins for the first time up close. And he remembers the paralyzing terror of understanding that Duke was utterly helpless to stop them.

"I don't think anybody realizes how good ACC players are until you have to coach against them," said Swenson, who went on to become the head coach at William & Mary. "That first season we're facing James Worthy, Michael Jordan, Buck Williams, and you could see right away we didn't have any players to compete with them."

Poor planning cost Krzyzewski on the recruiting front. Recognizing the difference in ability between his players and those at schools like North Carolina, Virginia and Maryland, Krzyzewski sought to rectify the situation overnight. He and his staff went after almost every big-name recruit in the country. Coming from Army, where his recruiting base was limited to players none of the top schools wanted, and into the ACC, which typically signs its share of the best high school players around, Krzyzewski was like a starving man unleashed on an all-you-can-eat barbecue buffet.

He went after too much, and made himself sick. Duke had received on-campus visits from as many impressive high school stars as almost any other college program, but signed none of them that first year.

"We were recruiting too many people," Krzyzewski said. "It was our fault. It wasn't bad luck or someone cheating us. Taking responsibility is the great lesson of West Point. They don't expect you to be perfect, only to be honest with yourself."

The truth was, the Blue Devils coaching staff was spreading itself too thin. Swenson spent thirty-four of forty-eight days on the road – during Duke's basketball season – looking at as many high school players as he could. The task was especially painful for Swenson, who was courting a young woman from Durham and didn't feel good about his future with her the longer he spent on the road. While Duke didn't sign a stellar class that year, at least not all was for naught; Swenson got engaged to his girlfriend that March.

It was the only victory of the recruiting season. Rather than focus on a handful of players, they went after everyone. And everyone went somewhere else. In just that first season alone, Duke lost out on players like Chris Mullin (who went to St. John's), Uwe Blab (Indiana), Rodney Williams (Florida), Jim Miller (Virginia) and Bill Wennington (also St. John's). The losses of Williams and Miller were especially painful. Krzyzewski traveled to Daytona Beach, Florida, to give a speech at the banquet honoring Williams' high school team, but Williams wasn't there.

He was in Gainesville, signing a scholarship with the Florida Gators.

The loss of Miller was equally disconcerting. Duke assistant Bob Dwyer drove through the night to the back-country town of Princeton, West Virginia, thinking he had an agreement with Miller, that Miller would sign a letter-of-intent with Duke once Dwyer got there. Before the meeting could take place, Miller's high school coach broke the news to Dwyer: Miller had changed his mind, and would be going, instead, to Virginia.

Krzyzewski and his chief recruiter, Swenson, regrouped and changed their tactics. Duke was a unique place, they reminded each other. The average grade-point average of the student body hovered near the 3.1 range – a high B average. Roughly ninety-three percent of the students graduated within four years. (Years later, Duke would add two courses to its mandatory number required to graduate, from thirty-two to thirty-four. Most schools require thirty-two.)

A 3.1 student-body grade-point average? A ninety-three

percent graduation rate in four years? Those were daunting numbers. Impressive, but daunting. Whereas some places with similarly high academic standards – Vanderbilt, Northwestern – struggled to pull this kind of tactic off, Krzyzewski and Swenson vowed to make the unique nature of student life at Duke a plus, not a minus, in recruiting. First, though, the Duke coaches knew they had to do a better job of targeting their talent pool.

"Of the top twenty-five players in the country, anywhere from thirteen to seventeen either just aren't interested in Duke, or we can't get them into school," Krzyzewski said.

Swenson said Krzyzewski may have been overly optimistic with his statistical analysis. "I remember years when as few as two or three of the top twenty-five players were admissible to Duke."

Whatever, Krzyzewski knew mass recruiting simply wouldn't work.

"(Duke's academic standards) reduce our pool, so we have to be very competitive for those kids who can play at this level and who we can get into school," he said. "We have to identify them real quick, because we don't have time to go out on the road and find out who they are. We have to know already. That makes us do our homework earlier."

Krzyzewski also found himself running into another problem: The Bobby Knight factor. Even as early as 1981, Knight was already wearing, like brass knuckles, a reputation as a sideline dictator – a winner, no question about it – but at what cost? Knight's reputation trickled down to Krzyzewski, the so-called Knight protege, the Knight disciple who surely, common thinking went, must practice what Knight preaches. A few years after he had been at Duke, Krzyzewski was confronted with that very idea by one of the top high school senior point guards in the country, Tommy Amaker. Amaker wanted to make sure he wasn't going to be playing for Bobby Knight South if he went to Durham.

Krzyzewski assured him he was no Bobby Knight. Amaker signed.

In 1981, Krzyzewski may not yet have been a terror on the recruiting trail, but he already had shown he could be as tough as anyone on the court. Too tough, some might say. Wake Forest coach Carl Tacy discovered that during the 1981-82 basketball schedule, Krzyzewski's sophomore season at Duke.

During a game at Cameron Indoor Stadium in Durham, a referee whistled one of Tacy's Demon Deacons, forward Guy Morgan, for setting an illegal pick. Enraged, Tacy raced down the sideline to confront the whistle-blower. Problem: On the way, Tacy bumped past Duke's Chip Engelland, who was standing on the sideline, waiting to throw the ball into play.

Krzyzewski erupted, sprinting down the sideline toward Tacy and Engelland, barking in Tacy's face to keep his hands off Duke's players. Tacy explained he was merely trying to get down the sideline to yell at the referee, and Krzyzewski, already known as a first-rate referee baiter, bought the explanation. Tacy apologized, and after the game he and Krzyzewski shook hands.

After the game, though, Krzyzewski still was somewhat miffed that an opposing coach would run into one of his players. "What was expected of me when I saw my player bumped? Just sit there and watch it happen? I don't think so," Krzyzewski said.

Duke closed Krzyzewski's first season with a blaze – a blaze the color of a red rose, actually – of glory. Before the season finale against North Carolina, ranked No. 11 in the country, Duke senior Gene Banks tossed red roses to the Cameron Indoor Stadium crowd to thank them for their support over his four-year career. Banks, an academic question mark when he committed because of a relatively low SAT score, had earned his degree in history in four years and delivered the commencement address to his fellow Class of 1981 graduates. Banks gave his classmates a different kind of presentation that day against North Carolina, tossing in an eighteen foot turn-around jump shot at the buzzer to force overtime. Then, in the extra session, he stuck in a rebound basket to beat the Tar Heels, 66-65.

There is a little secret behind Banks' eighteen footer that forced overtime. In the huddle before the final shot, Krzyzewski had called for the play to go to another Blue Devil. As the Blue Devils came out of the huddle, Banks stopped his teammates, now out of earshot of the bench, and demanded the ball be thrown to him instead. After the game, the students carried Banks off the court on their shoulders. Banks wrestled the public-address microphone away from the scorer's table and demanded that his mother come out of the crowd to join him.

———

After that highlight came the crash. Banks and Dennard graduated following the 1980-81 season, and Krzyzewski found himself living and dying with a nondescript group that included Tom Emma and Chip Engelland and Doug McNeely. They died, mostly. Duke went 10-17 in 1981-82, Krzyzewski's second season, eerily reminiscent of his last team at Army that went 9-17, and the worst mark at Duke since 1926-27, when the pre-Depression Blue Devils went 4-10 under coach George Buckheit. The season began with a double-overtime loss to Vanderbilt, and got worse. The mounting defeats took their toll on Krzyzewski, who, after Duke's 72-55 blowout loss to Princeton in December put the team's record at 1-4, slumped in the shower after the game and cried his eyes out. After that loss, a friend of the coach engraved a plaque with the date and score and an inscription that read "A POINT OF REFERENCE" to motivate Krzyzewski with the memory of where he, and the program, had been.

If Krzyzewski was saddened by the program's downward spiral, Duke fans were downright infuriated. They didn't blame Foster, who had done a poor job of recruiting before he left. They blamed Krzyzewski, who hadn't signed an impact player in his first recruiting season and whose head was the one they wanted on a platter. Butters wouldn't yield to the pressure, though, and gave his coach a vote of confidence. "He has a five-year contract," Butters told anyone who asked. "This is only the second year."

In the meantime, the Duke reputation was taking a beating. Duke, the school that had produced the Heyman-Mullins dynasty of the 1960s and the three-headed Spanarkel-Banks-Gminski monster of the 1970s, had become an ACC patsy by the early 1980s. The Blue Devils tied for sixth, ahead by a mere game of only Georgia Tech, in the ACC standings in 1981-82 at 4-10. They were a one-man show, Vince Taylor and the Middling Four, and Taylor's twenty-points-per-game scoring average just wasn't enough.

The next season was even worse. Duke slipped to a program-worst 3-11 record in the ACC, seventh place in the league ahead only of Clemson, and overall the record was 11-17. That included an utterly dreadful loss to Wagner, a school most Blue Devils fans probably didn't know existed before its basketball team came to Cameron Indoor Stadium in early January 1983 and left with an 84-77 victory.

Now in the NBA, Dennard was taking a verbal beating from the progeny of other ACC programs. He found himself having to defend Duke's honor, but he was fighting a battle with blanks for bullets. Duke lost four games by twenty points or more that season.

"It's very gratifying to say you're from Duke now, considering what they've accomplished, but it didn't come on a platter," Dennard said. "When I was with the Kansas City Kings and the Denver Nuggets (in the NBA),

I used to catch a lot of grief when we were losing to Wagner, Appalachian State, guys like that, let me tell you. They had some very difficult seasons. I played with (former North Carolina star) Phil Ford, Hawkeye Whitney (of N.C. State), Brook Steppe (of Georgia Tech), and they just rode me like a mule: "What's wrong with those Blue Devils? They've gone straight into the toilet.'

"That's the kind of stuff I was getting, and there wasn't a lot for me to say. What was I going to do, say, 'Wait 'till next year?' I had no idea what next year was going to bring. For all I knew it was going to get worse."

Trace the rise and fall – and subsequent rise again – of the Duke basketball program, and there is a clear low point, a definite spot where the program hit the bottom with a splat. The date was March 11, 1983. The place: the ACC tournament in Atlanta, Georgia. The opponent: Virginia.

The score: Virginia 109, Duke 66.

In the Duke hospitality suite overlooking the arena floor, Blue Devils boosters didn't bother lowering their voices as they discussed the need to fire Krzyzewski immediately and replace him with ... well, with anyone. Among the people in the suite who heard the grumblings was Mickie Krzyzewski, the coach's wife. After the game, she was too unhappy to join her husband for dinner. She stayed in the hotel room.

She missed one of the all-time best toasts ever heard at a Denny's restaurant.

It started like this. During the game Virginia center Ralph Sampson had feasted on a Duke front line that had no player taller than 6-8. After the game, after the 43-point pasting his team had handed to the Blue Devils, Sampson complained about the "dirty play" of the Duke forwards and center. Virginia coach Terry Holland made a similar complaint, a complaint that filtered its way to Krzyzewski in the other locker room.

"It's not their fault that they beat us by that score,"

Krzyzewski later said in *A March to Madness* by John Feinstein. "We were bad in the second half, really bad. But when you humiliate somebody that way, you don't rub it in by whining about a (Duke) freshman trying to push you around. (Besides) it was Ralph who threw the elbow."

Steamed, Krzyzewski found Holland in the tunnels underneath the coliseum leading to the different locker rooms, and had angry words for the Virginia coach. Holland could afford to be forgiving, and he was; he was a veteran ACC coach with job security and one of the best teams in the country. Krzyzewski, who was none of the above, still was furious after the game as a small gathering of Duke people ate dinner after midnight at an Atlanta Denny's.

The toast happened there. It was water, not wine, but it served its purpose. According to Duke legend, then-assistant sports information director Johnny Moore raised his water glass to the rest of the table and, in a moment of humility, proposed, "Here's to forgetting tonight."

Across the table, Krzyzewski raised his glass and made a correction:

"Here's to never forgetting tonight."

Virginia didn't beat Duke for seven years.

Chapter Four

COACH K, THAT'S WHO

In the midst of the worst season at Duke in more than half a century, hearing the bloodhounds baying for his job, Mike Krzyzewski changed forever the shape of Duke basketball with four white, eight-by-eleven sheets of paper in 1982.

On one sheet was the signature of Johnny Dawkins. On another, the signature of Mark Alarie. The third bore the scribble of Jay Bilas. The fourth, David Henderson.

The Fab Four.

Not that anybody was calling Dawkins, Alarie, Bilas and Henderson "The Fab Four," or anything else similarly hyperbolic, in 1982. Recruiting just wasn't followed that closely in those days. Less than a decade later recruiting experts would hang the tag "Fab Five" on a Michigan recruiting class of Chris Webber, Juwan Howard, Jalen Rose, Jimmy King and Ray Jackson. And indeed that Michigan recruiting class was a fabulous fivesome, the group starting as a quintet during its freshman season and leading the Wolverines into the Final Four. But back in 1982 there was no such clamoring for a nickname for the group Krzyzewski had signed. Recruiting experts existed, of course, but as one of them – Bob Gibbons of Lenoir, considered the foremost recruiting analyst in America – said years later, "People weren't listening to us as much as they do nowadays."

Which is why the howling for Krzyzewski's job wasn't quieted by the mammoth recruiting class he signed in 1982, his second full year on the recruiting trail at Duke. It was a class that was rated as the best in the country, and a class he wouldn't top at Duke for fifteen years – not that terribly many Duke fans knew what they had in that foursome. That would change soon enough, but not necessarily in 1982-83, Krzyzewski's third season at Duke and the inaugural season of the Dawkins-Alarie-Bilas-Henderson era. They were good enough to be Duke's best four players from their very first season together, but they weren't good enough to turn the program around in one year. Duke went 11-17 featuring a starting lineup of the four freshmen and one sophomore, a brutish, if not terribly talented, banger named Danny Meagher. As Alarie said years later, "It wasn't like we were getting a lot of leadership from Meagher. He was more of the bully of the group. We were learning, but we weren't winning."

And the Duke fans, they were whining – whining for Duke Athletic Director Tom Butters to replace Krzyzewski. Bunches of disgruntled Blue Devils backers wrote Butters angry letters about the coach and the program's direction since he had replaced Bill Foster. Butters saved the letters, but he did nothing about them. Why? Because he knew what others apparently did not. That Krzyzewski already had on his team the players that could turn the entire thing around.

———

Johnny Dawkins was the first.

"Johnny gave me a commitment," Krzyzewski said,

"when it wasn't fashionable to do that."

Dawkins was an unlikely looking savior, although, in hindsight, a savior is pretty much what he was for the Duke program. He was skinny, with knobby knees and bony shoulders slung close together, and the peculiar yet alluring shooting stroke of a left-hander, a rarity still in college basketball.

Dawkins was a 6-foot-3 scorer from the playgrounds of Washington, D.C., a player with moves no one at Sligo Creek Park near the nation's capital had seen before and moves not even Dawkins could replicate, much less explain where they had come from in the first place. He saw the basket, and he found a way to put the basketball in there. How did it happen? He wasn't so sure. "I've watched myself on film, and I have to admit sometimes I don't know where something came from," Dawkins said. "Whatever I do on the court is just a response to what I feel I have to do at that moment to get two points, or make a pass, or whatever it is I'm trying to do for the team."

About the only way Dawkins can put into words what he does in games is this: "I look at my defender's feet," he said. "You look to see which foot drops, which way he reacts, and you go the other way. If he drops back, you take the jumper."

The first time Krzyzewski saw Dawkins in a high school game, he knew he had to have him for Duke. A nice thought, but there was just one problem: Most of the other top programs in the country felt the same way. Everyone wanted Dawkins, because what he did on the court was simply this: score. Krzyzewski won Dawkins over with brutal honesty.

"He didn't promise me this or that like a lot of coaches were doing," said Dawkins, who in 1982 was the No. 1-rated recruit from the Washington, D.C. area. "He told me he was going to turn the thing around at Duke, and that he could use my help. He said it was going to be special and it would be challenging, and he asked me if I wanted to be a part of something that special and that challenging."

Yes, as a matter of fact, he did.

Dawkins came to Duke and, from his first day on campus, was the best player at school, and soon was one of the best players at the school – ever. Dawkins became the first player ever to lead the Blue Devils in scoring for four consecutive years, and he graduated with the most points in school history – 2,556 – a mark that still stood at the end of the twentieth century.

Alarie remembers his first gander at this particular goose.

"I had never seen Johnny play until our first pickup game at Duke," Alarie said. "He was just one of a kind, the most creative scorer that I had ever seen at our level. I never played against anybody like Johnny. He could always create something. He was the quickest, the most deceptive player I had ever seen. I knew I was going to have fun playing with him."

———

Mark Alarie was the second.

He made his commitment to Duke shortly after Dawkins had done the same, though the arrival of Dawkins had nothing to do with Alarie's desire to sign with a team coming off a 10-17 record in 1981-82. Alarie didn't look at Duke and see a dying dinosaur. He saw a sleeping giant, a program with great tradition, something that doesn't go away with just one poor season.

"I thought they had a lot of tradition at Duke," Alarie said. "The program was looking lean at the time, but even back then, Duke was one of the Top-10 programs of all time. I always thought of Duke as being a premier program, even then. It may have fallen on its face a little bit at times, but it was certainly top notch."

Alarie, a 6-foot-8 forward from Scottsdale, Arizona, never saw himself as a future millionaire in the NBA. He saw himself as a future investment banker or lawyer or something like that, and he narrowed his choice of schools accordingly. His final threesome was Stanford, Notre Dame and Duke – good basketball, and heavy on the academics. "Academics and basketball," Alarie said. "Those were my priorities, and in that order."

If Alarie seems to have been rather mature for a 17-year-old high school senior, maybe that's because he had been through so much already. Two years earlier, as a sophomore, his 42-year-old father had suffered a fatal heart attack while relaxing at home on the weekend. Alarie's younger brother, Chris, was born with cerebral palsy and spent most of his life in a wheelchair, unable to do the activities Mark would never take for granted.

"It's not like I spent my life trying to right this wrong that had been done to Chris," Alarie said years later. "But you learn to appreciate what you have when you see your little brother never getting out of his wheelchair. I mean, he came to every one of my games in high school, and he couldn't really focus on any one player. He was just there to support me. It was awesome."

The new Duke coach also appeared at a handful of Alarie's games at Brophy Prep in Scottsdale. Suffice it to say, Mike Krzyzewski's entrance into the school gymnasium did not have the effect that, say, the arrival of Bobby Knight or Dean Smith would have had.

"Frankly, no one in Arizona had heard of Coach K," Alarie said. "Definitely no one could pronounce his name out there. He was new to the scene, but very impressive as an individual. The meeting where he came out to Scottsdale to visit with me, he was the most passionate of the coaches that visited me. You could feel it in his voice, the way he communicates with his hands and eyes. You hear it, you know that he's speaking from his heart. Coach K's not, at least back then he wasn't, the most casual person. He's very focused, passionate. And he won me over. I chose Duke because it had the perfect combination of athletics and academics, and because of Coach K."

Alarie would average at least thirteen points a game all four years, become a two-time All-American and finish his career second only to his classmate, Dawkins, on the Duke scoring charts with 2,136 points, a total that, as of 1999, was still fifth all-time at the school.

"Mark Alarie has a great outside touch for someone his size," Krzyzewski said during Alarie's career. "I can't think of another 6'8" player in the country who can shoot like that."

Jay Bilas was the third.

The letters sealed it for him. More than fifteen years after he signed with Duke, Bilas was looking through an old trunk and came upon the letters, monstrously long, handwritten letters from Krzyzewski in the months the Duke coach was trying to convince the kid from California to sign with the Blue Devils. Krzyzewski wrote Bilas about life and love, about basketball, about anything at all. And Bilas, he was absolutely floored.

"I still have six or eight long, handwritten letters he wrote me when he was recruiting me, and they're something to see," Bilas said. "These were eight, ten pages, really personal stuff, and again, he wrote them in pen. That took time. That was impressive. No other coach did that for me."

Like Dawkins and Alarie, Bilas could have gone almost anywhere. A 6-foot-7 finesse forward, he was the top-rated player in California and regarded as one of the top fifty players in the country as a high school senior. With those handwritten letters Krzyzewski convinced Bilas that Duke should be his future home, but it was the tradition of the program, and the promise of the future, that piqued Bilas' interest in the first place.

"Now players are lining up to come to Duke," Bilas said in 1999, "but that wasn't the case when I was recruited. I have to be honest, if Coach K was at Wyoming State or some other place that's small with no tradition, I don't think I would have gone there. But if he was at UCLA, I would have gone to UCLA. If he was at Michigan, I would have gone to Michigan. He outworked everyone else when he recruited me, and I trusted him completely. When I was 18, basketball was the most important thing in my life, outside of my family. I'm not saying my priorities were correct or anything, but that's the way it was for me, and I suspect that's the way it is for most recruits. Basketball was the single most important thing in my life. And I trusted Coach K with that. That's how he gets his players. That's how he got me."

Bilas came to Duke as a lean, 215-pound forward and left as a 240-pound center with bulging biceps, if not bulging offensive statistics. Bilas did finish his career twenty-fourth on the all-time Duke scoring list with 1,062 points, a total that had slipped to thirty-eighth overall by the 1999 season. But he could have scored more in different circumstances, some feel.

"One thing that Jay had to deal with, he was a much more capable scorer than he got the chance to show," Alarie said. "He had to accept a role that didn't allow him to be a marquee-type player. He didn't get the kind of shots he would have had in any other program. We both got to school at 215 pounds, but when Jay found out he'd be asked to play center – that's just how it came down; it was going to be him or me – he bulked up to 235, 240 pounds, and he looked like Arnold Schwarzenegger. You could say Jay was a role player, but he was a very accomplished role player."

It was Bilas who guarded the top big men in the Atlantic Coast Conference. The Duke freshman who drew the ire of Virginia coach Terry Holland and 7-foot-4 center Ralph Sampson for "playing dirty" in that 109-66 loss in the 1983 ACC tournament? That was Bilas. Who guarded North Carolina's 6'10" Sam Perkins, Georgia Tech's 7'0"

John Salley and N.C. State's 6'11" Chris Washburn, all future NBA inside players? That was Bilas, who was at least three inches smaller than his man in almost every ACC game.

"I just did what Coach K asked of me," Bilas said. "I trusted him completely."

———

David Henderson was the fourth.

He was the least heralded member of that recruiting foursome to sign with Duke, but in some ways he was the most important. He was the glue, the fire, the attitude, an earlier version of Chris Carrawell, the gritty inner-city kid who inspired and fired Duke to the 1999 NCAA championship game.

Technically, the 6-foot-5 Henderson was a small forward, but there was very little small about him. He had the build of a linebacker to go with the explosiveness of a tailback. He was from the little North Carolina town of Drewry, where he had dreamed of playing for Dean Smith at North Carolina. That was the same dream of another player from the state, a 6'6" forward named Curtis Hunter, and Smith only wanted one player at that position. Smith chose Hunter.

Duke got Henderson. Krzyzewski was delighted. "I wanted David," he said. "David had those intangible qualities you look for in a kid, beyond whether he can score or rebound or any of that stuff that all of the top kids can do. David was a leader. David was a winner."

David, in hindsight, also was a better player than Curtis Hunter. In 121 career games with the Tar Heels, Hunter scored 502 points, a 4.2 average per game. Henderson, meanwhile, scored 1,570 points for the Blue Devils, a total that was twelfth all-time at Duke when he graduated, and twentieth in 1999. For his career, Henderson averaged 12.3 points a game. Above all else, Henderson elevated his game when the game itself was elevated. He earned All-ACC tournament honors during his career, and as a senior he was Most Valuable Player of the preseason Big Apple NIT in New York City.

"David's a great athlete," Alarie said. "He was the unheralded leader of our group. He was the toughest player we had in the class, and even back then I guess if you thought about it you could tell he was going to make a wonderful coach. He had the ability to communicate, and he had that passion that Coach K always had."

Indeed, Henderson and Dawkins both would become assistant coaches at Duke under Krzyzewski in 1997-98 and be there for the 37-2 season of 1999. But that's getting ahead of the story. There still was some losing to do.

After that 11-17 season in 1982-83, the first for the Dawkins and Co. youth movement, the players went their separate ways for the summer. Dawkins played on the United States' World University Games team that summer in Toronto. Alarie played on another team of U.S. college stars that toured Asia. Bilas and Henderson worked out informally with past Duke greats like Mike Gminski and Gene Banks in pick-up games at Cameron Indoor Stadium. When the foursome came back the following fall for their sophomore year, something dramatic had happened.

"We were so much better," Alarie said. "I played with guys like Brad Daugherty, Danny Manning and Karl Malone, and Johnny was basically on the team that would be the U.S. Olympic team the following year, so you know he had some great competition. When we came back to Duke, it was like, you looked around and said to yourself, "I don't remember him being that good. I don't remember him being that good, either. And I definitely don't remember me being this good.'"

That summer was big for another reason, too. It was the summer that saw the departure of Virginia center Ralph Sampson, the 7'-4" giant and National Player of the

Year who dominated the ACC for four seasons. With Sampson gone, Virginia, which had won at least a share of the last three regular-season ACC titles, had reverted back to mortality. It also helped that N.C. State, the surprising national champions from the previous season, had graduated stars Thurl Bailey and Sidney Lowe.

"That summer was like a catharsis for us," Alarie said. "We came back as sophomores with a lot more confidence, and then you looked around the ACC and some of the top teams had lost some talent, and you knew there was a chance for someone like us to move up the ladder."

Alarie had transformed himself that summer from a power forward with limited range to a big man with the outside touch of a shooting guard. "Duke is a very flexible system, but at the same time there are roles, and Coach K put me in the role of an inside banger my freshman year, because that's where I was needed most," Alarie said. "That summer there were no predetermined roles. I worked on what I wanted to work on, and I came back with a lot more confidence in my shooting."

As a freshman, Alarie had averaged thirteen points on 49.4-percent shooting from the floor. As a sophomore, those numbers improved to 17.5 points and 57.5 percent. The rest of the class had undergone similar transformations. Dawkins averaged 18.4 points, Henderson 13.5 – up from 9.1 – and Bilas had returned as a muscle-bound 240-pound behemoth.

Oh, and there was one other significant difference between Mike Krzyzewski's third and fourth teams at Duke. Finally, he had himself a point guard. Tommy Amaker would become for Krzyzewski what Krzyzewski himself had been for Bobby Knight at Army – intelligent, passionate, a demon on defense, an unselfish leader on offense. A coach on the floor, in other words. After being convinced by Krzyzewski during the recruiting process that the young Duke coach wasn't just a knockoff of his explosive mentor, Knight, Amaker signed – and as a freshman became the fifth starter, the right complement to the Dawkins-led foursome.

"Tommy kind of wrapped the whole thing up into a nice ball," Bilas said. "We had a lot of talent, but we lacked that one guy, that point guard, to distribute and lead and do all the things Tommy Amaker did for us. Also, Tommy allowed Johnny (Dawkins) to forget about distributing the ball and focus on the thing Johnny did best, which was score."

Amaker distributed, Dawkins, Henderson and Alarie scored, Bilas banged inside, and Duke began to win – win like it never had under Krzyzewski, and indeed, like it had rarely done since the days of Bubas in the 1960s. Duke won fourteen of its first fifteen games, its best start since the 1965-66 team that reached the Final Four for the last time with Bubas. The wolves howling for Krzyzewski's job had been quieted, but as it turns out they were quiet only as long as the winning continued. After that 14-1 start, it didn't. Duke lost its next four games, all in the conference, including three losses at Cameron Indoor Stadium. Three of the losses were by six points or less, but that was of little consequence. Duke fans were not happy. They began writing letters again to Athletic Director Tom Butters, though the tenor had changed somewhat. They no longer wanted to know why Krzyzewski couldn't get top-notch players. Now they wanted to know why he couldn't win with them, now that he had them. Krzyzewski had only one year left on his contract, the naysayers noted. Maybe a change was in order.

What the wolves needed was patience. Mike Krzyzewski was about to earn forever a place in the hearts of every Duke fan. And he was about to tick off the royal regime nine miles south on Highway 15/501.

The two go hand in hand, as you might imagine.

———

It might have been the most enjoyable loss Duke has

ever suffered against North Carolina. The final score was 78-73, but that's not why people remember the January 21, 1984 meeting between the Blue Devils and Tar Heels. They remember it because that was the day someone dared to speak out against Dean Smith, the czar of Atlantic Coast Conference coaches.

That someone was Krzyzewski.

The background: One week before the No. 1 Tar Heels visited Cameron Indoor Stadium, Duke had played host to Maryland, which had a player named Herman Veal, who had recently been accused of sexual misconduct. The Cameron Crazies were brutal to Veal, among other things throwing condoms onto the floor at his feet, their treatment so nasty that Duke officials warned them to clean up their behavior for the next game. The next game was North Carolina.

The key moment: Four minutes left, Duke leading 67-64. North Carolina's star center, Sam Perkins, was called for his third foul, and Smith popped off the bench to discuss the matter with the officials. From all accounts Smith wasn't trying to harangue the officials; rather, he wanted to clarify that Perkins was indeed the player they meant to call for the foul. But Smith's once-harmless intentions were gone when the referees, Mike Moser and John Moreau, apparently didn't see or hear him, and put the ball into play.

Smith, ignored, blew his top. He stalked down the sideline to the scorer's table and began pounding on it with his palm, trying to get the officials' attention. When that didn't work he demanded that the scoreboard operator, Tommy Hunt, sound the horn to stop play. No way, Hunt said.

Smith tried to sound the horn himself, but hit the wrong button. The result of his action dripped with irony for North Carolina bashers who love to whine that the Tar Heels get help from the officials. Instead of sounding the horn, Smith hit a button that gave his team 20 more

points on the scoreboard, which now read: UNC 84, Duke
67. By now, Smith wasn't the only person inside Cameron
Indoor Stadium who had gone berserk. So had the crowd,
the Duke bench and Krzyzewski. The Duke coach was
screaming at the officials to put a leash on Smith – i.e., hit
him with a technical foul – but the officials, who already
had lost control of the situation, refused.

North Carolina's Michael Jordan – maybe you've
heard of him – won the game for the Tar Heels with
three consecutive shots down the stretch.

Then it was Krzyzewski's turn to unload.

His face still red with anger, Krzyzewski stormed into
the postgame press conference room and, before he
would take a single question, began this way: "I want to
tell you something. When you come in here and start
talking about how Duke has no class (a reference to the
Herman Veal taunting the previous week), you'd better
start getting your stories straight – because our students
had class and our team had class. There was not a person
on our bench who was pointing a finger at the officials or
banging on the scorer's table ... You cannot allow people
to go around pointing at officials and yelling at them
without technicals being called. That is just not allowed.
So let's get some things straight around here and quit the
double standard that exists in this league, all right?"

Krzyzewski had publicly put a dunce cap on Dean
Smith's head.

Three days later, Duke extended Krzyzewski's original
five-year contract, which was down to its final fifteen
months, by another five years.

Coincidence? Possibly. Negotiations between Butters
and Krzyzewski had been held in the weeks leading up to
the North Carolina game. But if Butters had been holding
onto to any doubts about his young coach, they were alle-
viated when Krzyzewski stood up to Smith. "We offered
the first five years on what we thought he could do,"
Butters said. "Now, this five is on what I know he can do

and what he's in the process of accomplishing. He deserved it, he's earned it, and the university is extraordinarily pleased with him as a man and as a coach. For years I've been asked my yardstick on a coach, and Mike measures up to it."

Not that all Duke fans were equally convinced. After the contract extension was announced, Butters began receiving a handful of death threats. He also got a number of angry letters from Duke fans, inquiring about his sanity. "I still have the letters," Butters said years later. "Now I get letters from the same people, wanting to make sure I'm paying (Krzyzewski) enough."

———

Duke finished that 1983-84 season with a 24-10 record, a No. 14 national ranking and a spot in the NCAA tournament. The Blue Devils' climb up the mountain continued the next season, which they began ranked sixth in the country and which saw them never fall out of the Top 10. Duke ended the season on a disappointing note, however, losing in the second round of the NCAA tournament to unranked Boston College.

Still, Krzyzewski liked the future. He saw, in the upcoming 1985-86 season, a team led by four seniors – Dawkins, Alarie, Henderson and Bilas – and with a junior at point guard in Tommy Amaker. "We were much more together as a team," Krzyzewski said. "We were able to give Johnny Dawkins more freedom because of Amaker handling the ball. It freed (Dawkins) up to go to the boards, and he was also getting the ball at midcourt ready to score instead of having to set up the offense."

Indeed, Dawkins was ready to produce one of the best seasons in Duke history. His team was ready to do the same. In the meantime, Krzyzewski had gone back to the recruiting well and added two more key components.

Everybody wanted Danny Ferry, a 6'10" forward from DeMatha High near Washington, D.C., whom many analysts rated the No. 1 recruit in his senior class. Everybody included North Carolina, which targeted Ferry as its top priority of the high school class of 1985. If it was possible, Maryland wanted Ferry even worse. For Ferry's official recruiting visit to the Maryand campus, which was located a few miles from his home, Terrapins coach Lefty Driesell picked up Ferry in a limousine and took him to College Park Airport. There, Ferry and Maryland assistant coach Ron Bradley climbed into a small plane that flew over Ferry's house and then on to Cole Field House, the Terps' barn-shaped gymnasium. When Ferry looked down at Cole Field House, he saw a giant sign draped over the gym's roof proclaiming it to be "DANNY'S HOUSE."

If Lefty Driesell turned Ferry's visit into a carnival, Krzyzewski made Ferry's visit to Duke more like a weekend at home with family. Ferry and another Duke recruit, point guard Quin Snyder from the Pacific Northwest, spent their official visit to Durham with the Krzyzewskis, eating Mickie's cooking and watching Mike's television. But that wasn't the visit that wrapped up Ferry in the royal blue of Duke. No, that came a little later when he visited North Carolina. One night during his stay in Chapel Hill, Ferry went to a local nightclub with some North Carolina players. A handful of Duke players walked in. Ferry ended up hanging out with the Blue Devils, and a few weeks later, he signed with them.

Ferry would finish his career with 2,155 points, which was good for third on the all-time Duke charts. He was a two-time All-American and the 1989 National Player of the Year, as well as the first player in ACC history to finish a career with more than 2,000 points, 1,000 rebounds and 500 assists. No one in the ACC has ever scored more points in a game than Ferry's fifty-eight against Miami in

1988.

Ferry represented more than a basketball hybrid of the future, a player with the height of a center but the shooting ability of a guard. He represented to Krzyzewski the proof that Duke could go toe-to-toe with North Carolina in the recruiting wars and win – at least every now and then. "Danny Ferry was the first big-name guy that chose Duke over North Carolina," Krzyzewski said. "I'll remember him for that."

A year before Ferry signed, an offensively challenged high school forward had won over Krzyzewski with his defensive ingenuity. His name was Billy King. Krzyzewski knew he had to have King when he saw him during a high school camp one summer guarding future Georgetown star Reggie Williams, a pure scorer. King shut down Williams so thoroughly, he became known as "The Defender." Later, at Duke, the intelligent, handsome, engaging King would be nicknamed "Senator" for his can't-miss future in whatever field he chose. Just not basketball. The NBA wants its 6-foot-6 players to be able to score.

In college, though, King's defensive focus made him an ideal player for Krzyzewski, who believed his teams would win primarily with defense. King helped win more than his share of games, including a 70-61 victory against Notre Dame during his senior season when he held Fighting Irish All-American guard David Rivers to nine points on a shooting line that reads like a misprint: 3-for-27 from the floor. A few weeks later Temple All-American Mark Macon would go 6-for-29 against King, with seven air balls.

––––––––––

Ferry, a freshman, and King, a sophomore, were reserves on one of the best Duke teams of all-time, that 1985-86 bunch featuring Dawkins, Alarie and Amaker. That team began the season ranked No. 6 in the country and steadily rose to No. 1 by February. Only consecutive losses in mid-January, at North Carolina and Georgia Tech by a combined ten points, kept Duke from entering the NCAA tournament with a perfect record.

Dawkins would average 20.8 points per game, shoot 54.9 percent from the floor and 81.2 percent from the foul line, and be named National Player of the Year. Alarie, an All-American that season, averaged 17.2 points in an offense that was built around Dawkins, not himself. Krzyzewski and his staff always got a hoot over Alarie's ability to score his share of points anyway. "Alarie had an unbelievable work ethic, and he was the most efficient player we had," said Pete Gaudet, an assistant on that 1986 Duke team. "We would be in coaches meetings and start laughing at Alarie's stats. He would get something like nine shots in a game and still score eighteen points because he'd make seven of them and also get some free throws. He was great like that."

Duke nearly got derailed in the first round of that 1986 NCAA tournament, finding itself perilously close to becoming the first No. 1 seed to lose to a No. 16 seed. The underdog was Mississippi Valley State, the school that produced NFL star receiver Jerry Rice but had little in the way of basketball tradition. Still, if it weren't for the heroics of Dawkins, Duke very likely would have lost that game. "Johnny came up to me after the game and told me, when he was done with his playing career, he was going to want a job on my staff and that when he asked me for that job, he was going to remind me of this game," Krzyzewski said. "Johnny was fabulous. He carried us that day, there's no question about it, and without him we would have been in a lot of trouble."

Duke advanced to the Final Four with relative ease, its first under Krzyzewski and the first since Bill Foster had led the Blue Devils there in 1978, where it got past Kansas 71-67 to reach the national title game. With all that senior star power, Duke needed its apple-faced freshman, Danny

Ferry, to hold off the Jayhawks. It was Ferry, the only Duke reserve to score in the game (eight points), who hit the go-ahead basket in the final thirty seconds and then drew a charging foul with eleven seconds left to take away Kansas' last possession with a chance to tie the score.

Duke probably would have won its first national championship that 1986 weekend in Dallas had it not been for a Louisville freshman named Pervis Ellison, whose nickname – "Never Nervous" – was never more appropriate than it was for those forty minutes against the No. 1 Blue Devils. Ellison missed just four of fourteen shots from the floor and scored twenty-five points, with eleven rebounds, to rally Louisville from a second-half deficit to a 72-69 victory that left the Blue Devils' seniors stunned.

"I don't think any of us thought we weren't going to win the national championship that season," said Alarie, who had twelve points and six rebounds in the title game. "Our freshman year, frankly, we were just trying to survive. We started four freshmen and one sophomore that year. But when we were seniors, I mean, from the first day of practice, we all thought we could win the national championship. That was our goal, and as the season progressed and we were playing really well, it seemed more and more like something that we could achieve. When we didn't, it hurt so bad, I can't even describe it."

Alarie had no way of knowing that 1986 Duke team would be the one to start it all, the first of seven Final Four appearances over nine seasons that included two national championships. Years later, though, the contributions of that recruiting class from 1982 would be obvious. The big picture was even more attractive than the breakthrough spot in the 1986 national title game. The big picture, in fact, looked a lot like the center circle of Cameron Indoor Stadium on March 2, 1986, when the Blue Devils beat North Carolina in the home finale for that glorious recruiting class, and afterward, with students streaming from the bleachers to celebrate, the Fab Four met for a group hug.

"There's a sense of pride on all our parts, and I don't think Jay and David and Johnny would mind me speaking for them," Alarie said. "When an alum comes up to me at a Duke game today and says, 'You guys started the whole thing, you must be very proud,' well, I am proud. We downplay that some because it's as much a function of Coach K and the program as the players, but we certainly feel proud that we were Coach K's first Final Four team, and because of that, we know we did something special. We helped get everything started."

———————

Chapter Five

DARING THE DEAN

They have so much in common. They shared so much. Why they had to share such an apparent mutual animosity is ... it doesn't make any sense.

One of them coached at an Atlantic Coast Conference school in North Carolina about twenty-five miles west of Raleigh. The other also coached at an ACC school in North Carolina about twenty-five miles west of Raleigh. One took a program with great tradition and slowly, after some rocky early years, made that tradition even stronger. So did the other one. Their schools were located less than ten miles apart. Hell, there were even trivial things they shared in common. Not only did their daughters each take piano lessons – they had the same piano teacher. The most striking feature on both coaches' faces is their nose, which give each a pinched-off voice that sounds as if it has worked its way through a too-skinny pipe. So many things in common.

But Mike Krzyzewski coached at Duke.

And Dean Smith coached at North Carolina.

The calm before the storm. Though cordial before most games, North Carolina's Dean Smith and Coach K brought out the competitive best in one another.

And so they spent seventeen years, verbally, at each other's throat.

Maybe it does make sense, after all.

They have so much in common, and yet they are nothing alike. Mike Krzyzewski comes from a Polish-American neighborhood in Chicago, is quick with a quip and can relax and actually bask in the spotlight. Dean Smith comes from the plains of Kansas and, although he, too, can display a devastatingly quick sense of humor, he is reluctant to give away too much to anyone outside of his basketball family and personal family. Krzyzewski plays tennis, loathes golf. Smith is an avid golfer who practiced his putting in hotel rooms while on the road. At Army, Krzyzewski played college basketball at one of the least prestigious basketball programs in the country. Smith played at Kansas, a college basketball landmark that played for the national championship when he was there in the 1950s. Krzyzewski's Duke teams play with freedom on offense, his point guards allowed to read the opposing defenses and react, while Smith's Tar Heels were more rigidly structured on offense, to the point where a star point guard such as Ed Cota had to look over to the bench almost every time up the court to get the play call from Smith.

There's more. Krzyzewski is a Republican, Smith a Democrat. When Krzyzewski met Republican President George Bush after Duke's 1991 national championship and Bush said he hoped to see Krzyzewski in the White House the next year as well, Krzyzewski answered, "I hope to see you, too." Alas, Bush was defeated in the 1992 election by Bill Clinton, who visited the Duke locker room after the 1994 national championship game loss to Arkansas. When Clinton later sent Krzyzewski an autographed picture of their meeting, the Duke coach reportedly put the photo in a drawer. Smith, meanwhile, is a liberal who, in 1959, helped integrate a Chapel Hill lunch counter by sitting next to a black patron. That's not meant to imply

Krzyzewski wouldn't have done the same if given the chance. It is only meant to highlight the fact that two men who would clash at least two times every year from 1980 to 1997 don't even vote the same way on election Tuesdays, for crying out loud.

Krzyzewski and Smith faced each other forty-five times – Smith's Tar Heels won thirty of those meetings – and they clashed from their first game. Yes, their very first one. It was the third game of Krzyzewski's Duke coaching career, that 78-76 loss to North Carolina in the Big Four Tournament in 1980. The Tar Heels had the ball with the clock running out when Smith made the mistake of thinking the final horn had sounded. As he ran over to shake Krzyzewski's hand, Smith ran headlong into this stinging reprisal from the rookie Duke coach: "The damn game's not over yet, Dean!"

It went from there.

Forty-four more times it went, Duke and North Carolina battling it out under the most intense scrutiny of any sporting event in the state. They played each other as many as four times a year some years, what with the now-defunct preseason Big Four Tournament and also occasional meetings in the ACC tournament, usually in the semifinals or championship game of that event. Not that playing each other over and over in pressure-cooker games necessarily had to turn Krzyzewski and Smith against one another. In some rivalries, the coaches remain in the background. The Nebraska-Oklahoma football games of the 1970s, for example, rarely revolved around the animosity of Huskers coach Tom Osborne and Sooners coach Barry Switzer, because no such animosity was evident.

It was with Krzyzewski and Smith.

It began with that first game in the Big Four Tournament, in 1980, after which Krzyzewski was asked how it felt to coach against someone of Smith's stature. "I can coach, too," Krzyzewski answered. Another early highlight was the 1984 "double standard" comment from Krzyzewski, which let everyone know – most of all, Dean Smith – that the young Duke coach wouldn't cower in the presence of the Tar Heels' legend.

In 1989, the students at Duke's Cameron Indoor Stadium taunted one of North Carolina's star players, J.R. Reid, with signs reading, "J.R. Can't Reid" – clever maybe, but absolutely inaccurate. Reid was not an unintelligent person, on or off the court. Smith, seeing a racial backdrop to the signs, went out of his way to mention that Reid's standardized test scores coming out of high school were better than those of two white players at Duke, Danny Ferry and Christian Laettner, whom Smith also had recruited (and therefore was privy to their test scores). Such a disclosure was technically illegal, since the Buckley Amendment prohibits schools from talking about students' grades. But that's not why Smith's remark infuriated Krzyzewski. Krzyzewski simply didn't appreciate it that Smith had embarrassed two of his players just so Smith could build up Reid. Krzyzewski let Smith know it, too.

That squabble set up the 1989 ACC tournament championship game one week later in Atlanta. North Carolina would go on to win its first tournament championship in seven years, 77-74, but only when Ferry's 75-foot three-point heave at the buzzer hit the back of the rim. The hottest fireworks came earlier, when North Carolina 6-foot-11 forward Scott Williams drew the wrath of Krzyzewski for a series of what Krzyzewski felt were unnecessarily violent fouls. Krzyzewski turned to Williams after one and yelled, "Don't foul so hard!"

Smith, hearing this, snapped to attention and yelled at Krzyzewski, "Don't talk to my players!"

Krzyzewski's response to Smith: "?@#! you!"

This wasn't finished. A few days later, the NCAA tournament selection committee seemingly did a disservice to North Carolina, sending the Tar Heels away from the East

regional – the regional commonly reserved for the
dominant ACC team every year – and putting them in the
same Southeast regional with a red-hot Michigan team.
Michigan would go on to defeat North Carolina in a Sweet
Sixteen game, while Duke, which had been sent to the
East regional, had a relatively easy road all the way to the
Final Four. Before the tournament began, Smith complained about being sent out of "the natural region." On
his own, Krzyzewski soon volunteered a snide remark
about "natural regions, whatever the hell that means."

In 1996, Duke walk-on Jay Heaps, an All-American
soccer player, was excessively rough with a foul on
North Carolina star guard Jeff McInnis, knocking McInnis
onto the press table. McInnis screamed at Heaps and
was called for a technical foul, his second of the game,
meaning automatic ejection. As McInnis headed for the
North Carolina locker room, the Cameron Crazies
rewarded him with the rhythmic chant, "?@#!-hole, ?@#!-
hole." Smith, still seething after the game, made what
seemed like a condescending remark, saying he was sure
the "esteemed" Duke faculty wouldn't condone the
behavior of the Duke student section.

Three days later Krzyzewski entered the fray, asking
Smith to mind his own business and pointing out,
somewhat condescendingly in his own right, that the
Duke students had merely "made an accurate comment
about McInnis."

And so it went. Krzyzewski against Smith. Smith against
Krzyzewski. Before it was all said and done, the things
they would do to each other went beyond competition.
Some of it bordered on petty. When Krzyzewski left his
team in the middle of the 1994-95 season with his back
and exhaustion problems, every ACC coach wrote a letter
or telephoned – or both – to show their concern and
support. Every coach but one, that is. While Georgia Tech
coach Bobby Cremins was calling so often that
Krzyzewski's wife, Mickie, finally had to ask him to stop,
Dean Smith, the coach eight miles down the road, never

inquired at all.

Krzyzewski would return the favor. In 1997 when Smith won his 877th career game, breaking Kentucky icon Adolph Rupp's all-time record for victories by a college basketball coach, every ACC coach called or wrote to congratulate Smith. Every coach but one, that is. That out of his system, Krzyzewski later was magnanimous when Smith announced his retirement about six months down the road, sending flowers not only to Smith, but to Smith's wife, Linnea, as well.

"You have to stand up at certain times," Krzyzewski said. "When someone is established in a business or sports, other people can't just buckle under to that person all the time. The perception that it's something against Dean Smith is wrong. It's something for Duke, and what we're trying to do. People would love to have us really hate one another. But, you know, there aren't too many people I hate. He's one I respect. I like him. But when you compete, you compete."

Krzyzewski has competed with Smith like no coach in the ACC ever has. Others constructed teams that could stand up to Smith's coldly efficient Tar Heels for periods of time – N.C. State's Norm Sloan in the early 1970s and Jim Valvano in the early 1980s; Duke's Bill Foster in the late 1970s; Maryland's Lefty Driesell in the early 1970s and again in the early 1980s; Wake Forest's Dave Odom in the mid-1990s. But none was able to sustain it for as long a period of time as Krzyzewski, who pulled his program even with Smith's Tar Heels in 1985, and kept it there until Smith retired after the 1997 season. For that, Krzyzewski earned Smith's respect as well.

"Mike has what we call 'a program' going," Smith said in 1991. "He's done an unbelievable job of recruiting. But the big thing I think for them was their four wins that propelled them into the Final Four (in 1986, 1988, 1989 and 1990). I know we've been to the final eight six times in the past ten years, but that doesn't mean anything. There's something magic about making the Final Four.

That's what people perceive and that's what gets the attention. Those four wins have been essential in sustaining their program, and with their recruiting and Mike's leadership, they're going to be there for a long time."

Krzyzewski, and Duke, on a par with North Carolina for a long time to come? Fitting. Duke and North Carolina had already been rivals a long time. Even before Dean Smith ever got to town.

———————

For years the rivalry wasn't much of a rivalry. Duke may have introduced the game collegiately in the state of North Carolina, but the Tar Heels were the first to perfect it. From 1921 to 1928, North Carolina never lost to Duke, winning sixteen consecutive meetings. It wasn't until Eddie Cameron became Duke's coach in the 1930s that the scales began to even out. By the 1950s, the rivalry was in full bloom.

That much was obvious in the early 1950s, when the Cameron Crazies used to taunt North Carolina coach Frank McGuire by loading up their hair with lard and pulling it back tight against their scalps, and by dressing in silly ties because McGuire liked his flamboyant neck wear. When Duke won eight consecutive games against North Carolina in those years, Duke players also mocked the Tar Heels coach by dribbling close to the North Carolina bench and taunting McGuire.

By the time Vic Bubas had become Duke's coach in 1960, the Blue Devils and the Tar Heels were such enemies that Bubas' daughters once refused to eat a birthday cake because the icing was too similar to North Carolina's school colors. That anti-North Carolina act by two young girls drew national attention.

And then Duke and North Carolina began recruiting the same players.

What had been an emotional, passionate rivalry started to turn ugly in 1960 when North Carolina and Duke vigorously courted Art Heyman, the 6-foot-5 forward from

Once upon a time, Coach K was a fiery point guard for Bobby Knight at West Point.

Coach K gives a thumbs down to a referee's call during a 1986 game against Kansas

Coach K led his 1986 team to the first Final Four of his Duke tenure.

Coach K and the four women in his life, c. 1990 (from left): wife, Mickie and daughters Lindy, Jamie (bottom) and Debbie.

Christian Laettner was one of the most talented, and temperamental, players ever to suit up for Coach K.

Krzyzewski shows his displeasure during a second-round loss to Virginia in the 1994 ACC Tournament.

Although they arrived with two national championships under their belt, Duke lost in the 1994 national title game to Arkansas. Krzyzewski is pictured here with senior guard Marty Clark.

Coach K and Steve Wojciechowski share a hug after Duke's 77-75 victory against UNC in Wojo's final game at Cameron Indoor Stadium.

Coach K shows his fury over the physical play of Clemson that left Duke co-captain Trajan Langdon bleeding on the floor at Cameron Indoor Stadium in 1999.

Coach K doesn't have much of a poker face when he stalks the sideline, as shown here against Maryland in 1999.

Coach K savors a victory against North Carolina in the 1999 ACC Tournament championship game.

After ripping through the season 16-0 in the ACC, Duke wins the 1999 ACC Tournament title with ease. L-R: Nate James, Shane Battier, Krzyzewski, Chris Carrawell, Trajan Langdon, William Avery, Elton Brand.

Coach K keeps a close eye on his team's progress early in his career at Duke.

Assistant coach Quin Snyder tries to calm Coach K during the 1999 East Regional title game.

Going to the Final Four! Coach K celebrates the final moments of an 85-64 victory against Temple in the 1999 East Regional final, with point guard William Avery.

Two heads are better than one – Coach K and assistant coach Quin Snyder at the 1999 Final Four against Michigan State.

Coach K gives Shane Battier (middle) and William Avery (left) last minute instructions before a 1999 Tournament game against SW Missouri State.

Coach K talks to a referee during the 1999 ACC championship game against North Carolina.

Coach K and Connecticut's Jim Calhoun share a laugh one day before Calhoun's Huskies stunned the Blue Devils to win the 1999 national championship.

This game – the 1999 national championship against Connecticut – had a thumbs-down result for Duke.

Coach K makes his opinion known, and the referee responds in kind –
technical foul.

Surrounded by his 1999 team, including seven former high school All-Americans, during a timeout in the game at N.C. State.

Long Island. Heyman signed a scholarship to play for the Tar Heels, but on his final visit to Chapel Hill before enrolling, Heyman had to separate his stepfather and McGuire from fighting after his stepfather said something about McGuire running "a factory." Angered by the incident, Heyman ended up at Duke, although he later would say North Carolina had a chance at getting him until the very end. "If Duke hadn't been there to pick me up at the airport," Heyman told *Sports Illustrated* in 1995, "I would have just gone down the road (to North Carolina) and started there."

As it happens, two of Heyman's friends from New York, Larry Brown and Doug Moe, went to North Carolina. They're probably not friends any more, Heyman and those guys. In a 1960 freshman game between the Tar Heels and Blue Devils, Moe spat on Heyman. The next season, with everyone now on their respective varsity teams, Brown and Heyman got into a fight after a spirited foul by Heyman – by the way, Brown and Heyman would have been roommates had Heyman followed through on his commitment to North Carolina – and their fight flowered into a full-scale brawl that included fans and cheerleaders from both teams and required almost ten police officers to break up. A North Carolina fan swore out an assault warrant against Heyman for Heyman's fight that day with a North Carolina cheerleader. Heyman would later say that he felt he spent the rest of his career being followed by private detectives funded by particularly zealous North Carolina fans, and indeed he may have been; how else do you explain his arrest a few years later for "transporting a woman across state lines for immoral purposes" into Myrtle Beach, South Carolina? Who knew that Heyman was even at the hotel? Private detectives, Heyman felt, that's who.

The Duke-North Carolina rivalry only grew. Dean Smith, who had been hung in effigy by Tar Heels fans after an 8-9 debut season in 1962, may have saved his job the next year by convincing hotshot recruit Larry Miller of Catasauqua, Pennsylvania, to sign with North Carolina instead of Duke, which was coming off a spot in the 1963 Final Four and already was in the habit, under Bubas, of getting every potential recruit it sank its teeth into.

Bubas got even in 1969, his last season at Duke. His final recruiting coup was Dick DeVenzio, a guard whom Smith badly, badly wanted to sign. The next season, when Duke beat North Carolina 91-83, Smith said, "This game was decided a year ago when Dick DeVenzio decided to go to Duke."

Back and forth it went. Smith lashed back in 1976, signing Mike O'Koren when everyone in Durham was under the assumption O'Koren was a done deal Duke signee. O'Koren, a 6-foot-6 forward from Jersey City, New Jersey, had been a high school teammate of then-Blue Devils point guard Jim Spanarkel, but on signing day he stunned the Blue Devils by signing with North Carolina instead. That probably explains the Cameron Crazies' cruelty toward O'Koren over the following four years. Every time North Carolina came to Cameron Indoor Stadium, the Duke students greeted O'Koren, who had his share of acne, with signs like, "OXY-1000 POSTER CHILD." For his part, O'Koren wanted to beat Duke so badly, especially in Cameron Indoor Stadium, that he once collapsed from heat exhaustion after a game there.

Duke's students seemed to save their best stuff for the hated Tar Heels. On one game day against North Carolina, the Duke student paper left blank an entire page, save for the caption, "This big, useless white space was put here to remind you of Eric Montross" – the Tar Heels' 7-foot center. Duke students once sympathized with North Carolina guard Steve Hale's collapsed lung by chanting at him, "In-Hale, ex-Hale, in-Hale."

North Carolina's students get into the rivalry as well. During the 1992 regular season, a group of North Carolina students broke into Cameron Indoor Stadium and stole, from a glass-enclosed case in the lobby, Duke's 1991 Final Four trophy, plus a basketball and a rim net from that national championship weekend. The missing prizes appeared twenty-four hours later, decorating the Old Well on the North Carolina campus, with a note that read, "I will not snatch Duke's priceless championship memorabilia" – written over and over, one hundred times.

At times the relationship between the schools seems almost incestuous, given the animosity between the two. One of the greatest players in North Carolina history, Phil Ford, played his final home game as a senior against Duke overcome with such emotion that Duke players saw him literally crying on several trips down the court. Ford scored a career-high thirty-four points that day, and North Carolina won 87-83. A decade later he was married – at Duke Chapel. There's more. Duke's Mark Alarie scored the first basket ever in the Dean Smith Center. A former chancellor at North Carolina, Paul Hardin III, has two degrees from Duke, while a former Duke president, Terry Sanford, has two degrees from North Carolina. The name of the Tar Heels' longtime radio announcer is Woody Durham. The exit you take from Highway 147 to get to Duke's campus is Chapel Hill Street.

Given all that, Krzyzewski adamantly hopes the schools never meet in the national championship game. "I can live with losing to any school," he said. "But what would happen in this area, people-wise, if one of us beat the other in the championship game ... that I wouldn't wish on anybody, it would be so horrible."

At times, it is bad enough just when one team loses in a big game – and not necessarily to the other. Look what happened in 1999 alone. After North Carolina was upset in the first round of the NCAA tournament by thirteenth-seeded Weber State, Duke students poured out of their dorms and used wood benches around campus for a bonfire, a celebration normally reserved for a Duke victory against the Tar Heels – not a Weber State victory against the Tar Heels. A few weeks later, when Duke lost in the national championship game to Connecticut, Tar Heels fans flooded Franklin Street, the main strip along campus, and partied so hard that local police officers were called to keep the peace.

After one North Carolina victory against Duke in the mid-1980s, Krzyzewski's oldest daughter, Debbie, was hounded the next day at junior high by a gaggle of class-mates – North Carolina fans – who followed her around the halls, jostling her and taunting her. One teacher even gloated, "Go Heels!" in the margins of one of Debbie's papers.

Debbie Krzyzewski got her revenge years later. By then a sophomore at Duke, Debbie was dating a sophomore from North Carolina who sat with the Krzyzewski family during a Duke-North Carolina game and couldn't refrain from cheering for the Tar Heels after a dunk by Rick Fox. Bad news for the boyfriend: Mike Krzyzewski had chosen that moment to toss a glance at his family. Worse news for the boyfriend: Debbie soon broke up with him.

In 1993, Chris Collins signed with Duke over North Carolina. Collins, the son of former Chicago Bulls coach Doug Collins, was once a ball boy for the Bulls and had always enjoyed a tight relationship with Bulls star Michael Jordan, a former star at North Carolina. When Jordan learned of Collins' choice of college, he draped an arm around Collins and said, "You'll always be my boy, but now that you're a Dookie, I can't talk to you any more."

Maybe Jordan was kidding. Maybe not. The rivalry does strange things to people. Supernatural things, even. After he forced overtime with a late jumper and then helped Duke beat North Carolina 66-65 in the extra session, Duke senior Gene Banks said, "It was the closest I've ever felt to God. And I don't mean that to be blasphemous."

As if there weren't enough reasons for the Blue Devils and Tar Heels to clash, fate apparently seems to want it this way, too. In 1986, when North Carolina opened the state-of-the-art Dean Smith Center on its campus, the first game was against Duke. Everything in the place seemed to be glorious; everything, that is, except for one seat in one section. Mickie Krzyzewski's seat was broken. Gallantly, the wife of the Duke coach refused when North Carolina officials offered to find her another chair.

Years after they left college for the NBA, former Duke star Christian Laettner and former North Carolina star Jerry Stackhouse landed on the same team, the Detroit Pistons. One night in 1999, flying back to Detroit after a game, Laettner and Stackhouse were playing cards. Then they were fighting. The Blue Devil and the Tar Heel. Everyone understood.

Coach K and Dean didn't get along? Welcome to the Atlantic Coast Conference, where passions about basketball sometimes are thicker than common sense. And around no coach did that unfortunate truth seem to revolve more than Smith, whose incredible success in the conference – thirty-four consecutive years in the ACC's top three, including regular-season championships in half those years – grated on his coaching foes as much as his personal and/or coaching style.

N.C. State coach Jim Valvano often told the story of his first week on the State campus in 1980. He was getting his hair cut when the barber said he hoped Valvano would have better luck in Raleigh than his predecessor, Norm Sloan. "Wait a minute," Valvano said to the barber. "Didn't Sloan go 27 0 and win the national championship one year?"

"Yes," the barber answered, "but imagine what Dean Smith would have done with that team."

Maryland's Lefty Driesell bickered for years with Smith, once angrily calling a less-than-complimentary postgame comment Smith had made after a North Carolina victory in 1982 "a bunch of crap." The next year,

Driesell wrote Smith a terse letter, telling Smith not to bother with the pregame or postgame handshake the next time the teams played, because Driesell wanted no part of it. When Driesell followed through on his threat and stood up the waiting Smith after the Terps' next game against the Tar Heels, another North Carolina victory, normally mild-mannered Tar Heels assistant Bill Guthridge chased down Driesell in a corridor outside the locker room and had to be restrained by onlookers from going after the Maryland coach.

Of course, Driesell practically loved Smith compared to the way N.C. State's Sloan felt about the North Carolina coach. Driesell used to joke that for years he thought Smith's name was "that G**-damn Dean" because Sloan was always calling Driesell in his office at Maryland, shouting, "Do you know what that G**-damn Dean just did?"

Years later, nearly a decade after Krzyzewski's "double standard" remark, the next ACC coach to take on Smith was Clemson's Rick Barnes, a tough, cocky and gifted coach whose teams played every bit as physically as did their football counterparts at Clemson. In 1995 Smith objected to Clemson's style during a game at the ACC tournament, and Barnes nearly went after him right there on the sideline. A year later, when Smith appeared to advise a Clemson player how not to foul the Tar Heels too much – "Stop playing with your hands," Smith told a Clemson player, "you're a good player. Play with your feet." – Barnes told Smith to mind his business. The two exchanged verbal swipes through the press for a few more days before being called to ACC Commissioner Gene Corrigan's house for a private meeting to air their differences. The meeting was little help. Smith showed up with a tape of Clemson's players. Barnes showed up with four tapes.

Even Krzyzewski's predecessor, Bill Foster, took his share of jabs at Smith, once saying, "I always thought it was Naismith who invented the game, not Dean Smith."

On the whole, meanwhile, ACC coaches had been publicly feuding since the days of N.C. State's Everett Case and North Carolina's Frank McGuire. The highlight of their running feud was when McGuire accused Case of running up the score in a seven-point victory in 1954, Case responded with laughter, and McGuire responded with the declaration, "I am declaring open war against Everett Case."

Yes, coaches in the ACC had done their share of bickering before Smith and Krzyzewski came along. Smith and Krzyzewski just took it to a new level.

They were not friends. They didn't get together in the offseason for a cup of coffee or a beer, nor did they have dinner when they were on the road together recruiting or attending an NCAA coaches function. Mike Krzyzewski and Dean Smith simply had little use for one another, even if their daughters had the same piano teacher, even if their wives occasionally would see each other out and chat for several minutes, even if their players played together all summer and hung out at the same parties during the season.

"Dean and I are different," Krzyzewski said, "and that's what makes it interesting."

It doesn't hurt that Krzyzewski liked to take his little shots at the North Carolina coach. Krzyzewski once tried to diffuse any talk of a personal rivalry between himself and Smith by saying he and Smith got along. But Krzyzewski couldn't help himself. With a smile, he added, "But I wouldn't go over to his house and smoke cigarettes."

Smith, at the time, was a smoker, though he has since quit. Krzyzewski never has smoked.

Smith wants to beat Duke so badly, he once made a rare admission that he enjoyed a victory at Cameron Indoor Stadium more than almost anywhere else. "At

Cameron Indoor Stadium, and this shows my immaturity, I have more fun by shutting up the student body with a win," Smith said. "That's immature, but I have to admit sometimes it's more of a satisfaction walking off the court there after a win. The players and coaches say, 'Nice game,' but you ought to hear what the students call me, see the anger in their faces. So, yes, it is better."

Smith and Krzyzewski have waged their wars at Cameron, and at the Smith Center in Chapel Hill as well, but on the other hand they have gotten along away from the court and clearly there is a mutual respect there. They confer about various proposed legislation that will affect college basketball. They were for the most part cordial before games during the ritual coaches' handshake. And one year, before their annual game at Cameron Indoor Stadium, Krzyzewski called Smith on game day – two times, in fact – to explain a change in the national anthem format to make sure the Tar Heels were prepared and not potentially embarrassed by the schedule change.

Krzyzewski and Smith once found themselves in adjacent seats on a plane flight to a coaching clinic in 1996. They talked, according to Smith, about "mostly basketball," it was breathlessly reported later.

And they did play tennis once at a Nike retreat for its coaches under contract. Smith and Southwestern Louisiana's Marty Fletcher played Krzyzewski and Georgia Tech's Bobby Cremins. Although he hadn't played tennis in almost twenty years, Smith and his team won. "I think Cremins threw it to help me out," Krzyzewski later said, smiling. "Let's put it this way: I am not as much a better tennis player as (Smith) is a much, much better golfer. I've never taken golf lessons. With my back, I've played golf three times, nine holes, with my wife, when no one's on the course. I mean, that's his game. Tennis is not his game."

Later at that retreat, Krzyzewski and Smith almost

seemed to connect. Smith made the effort. Krzyzewski seemed to appreciate it. "I don't know if he was doing humanitarian work throughout the Nike trip, but it was like he was doing the decathlon," Krzyzewski said. "He did everything on that trip. He was even playing cards with the guys at night. We had to tell him to slow down."

At times, like during basketball games, they can be at each other's throats. And at other times, when there is more time for reflection, Krzyzewski and Smith can be downright sappy when talking about the other.

From Smith: "Certainly I admire the job Mike has done as a basketball coach and as a representative of Duke University. In recruiting we say nice things about Duke, and I think they say nice things about us. I think, being this close, we've done extremely well. When I say 'this close,' you have to work at the relationship. It's not like we're professors of philosophy at North Carolina and Duke. Because of media interest in intercollegiate basketball in the area, we have to work at it. Some of our fans and some of their fans can be really ... like their identification is wrapped up in it, and that's too bad. It's a game."

Indeed, both coaches have had garbage thrown on their lawns, presumably by gloating fans of the other school, after losing to their nearby rival.

"I think there are shots taken back and forth (between me and Smith) and some of it I think is the result of different styles. But I don't think that's bad," Krzyzewski said. "I think you have to be who you are. If I could change one thing with people in our area, it would be this – don't, as a fan of Duke or North Carolina, try to compare the two of us. Don't try to figure out that somebody doesn't do something as well on Tuesdays or somebody won more national championships in fewer years. Those are irrelevant things.

"Who's best? I don't think there will ever be a 'best' in coaching, but there'll be 'one of the best' – and I'm just talking about records – and he is definitely in that category and I think I've been in it and hopefully I can continue to be in it. He's done it for a long period of time. What I would like is – just accept the fact that, if you're a Duke fan, (Smith) has done it pretty darn well, one of the best, and if you're a Carolina fan, accept the fact that for the time, we've done it pretty darn well, and it's been one of the best.

"There's too much negative stuff. It doesn't make me feel good if I hear a Duke fan, or any other fan, say negative stuff about a guy who has won over 850 games."

———————

What they did, Dean Smith and Mike Krzyzewski, was bring out the best in one another. It is that simple. Smith had been winning games at a record pace for two decades before Krzyzewski was hired in 1980 – but Smith didn't win a national championship until several years after Krzyzewski was hired by Duke. And Smith didn't win his second national title, in 1993, until Krzyzewski had tied him with one NCAA title in 1991, and surpassed him with a second championship for Duke in 1992. Smith downplays the timing of it all, of course, not wanting to give Krzyzewski any credit for North Carolina's post-Krzyzewski surge. "You can't say we did well because someone else was doing well and we wanted to keep up," Smith said. "Our success has nothing to do with anyone else."

They essentially turned the ACC into a two-team league – Duke and North Carolina and the six, then seven, dwarves – for the second half of the 1980s and most of the 1990s. Sure there were interlopers, teams like Wake Forest and Clemson and N.C. State sneaking out a regular-season title, but for the most part the rest of the conference was trying to keep up with Duke and North Carolina – who, in the meantime, were chasing each other's tails like two very big dogs running in one very small, tight circle.

In the seventeen seasons Krzyzewski and Smith competed, from 1981 to 1997, Duke and North Carolina combined to send fourteen teams to the Final Four, played in eight national championship games and won four national titles. "We've had great basketball here," Krzyzewski once said in the middle of that stretch. "In an environment of excellence, we've made each other better. There's no place like it in the world. No place.

"Just beating Carolina would be a ridiculous goal. You being really good should be your goal. You might defeat Carolina in a basketball game, but you're not going to shut down their basketball program. It's a hell of a program. It's like owning a restaurant when there's another one across the street. You're going to make sure you don't have any bad days, any bad meals."

For seventeen years there were very few bad days, very few bad meals. Only once since Krzyzewski got the Duke program rolling in 1984 did either team fail to reach the NCAA tournament, and that was the 1994-95 season, for Duke, when Krzyzewski was sidelined after twelve games – with a 9-3 record, by the way – because of a bad back and exhaustion. That break in the action seems to have given Krzyzewski an even greater appreciation for what Smith accomplished in the cauldron that is ACC basketball.

"I think longevity is commendable in any position, but longevity with high excellence in your work is something that has to be admired," Krzyzewski said. "It has to be used as an example for people, not just in our profession but in other professions as well. I respect what (Smith) has done over that long period of time and what he has accomplished. I think he's done it in a very good way.

"I know how competitive he is. This is what I do: I admire the fact that he is that competitive after that period of time. Fans or whatever have no idea how competitive you have to be and what you have to put into it to achieve a championship. And after you've done it, after you've won an ACC championship or gone to a Final Four or won a national championship, after you've done it and then done it again and you still go after it in a manner like he has – that's unique. I think I admire that more than anything about him."

———————

Chapter Six

THIS IS NO FLUKE

By 1986, Duke and Coach Mike Krzyzewski had arrived. A Final Four? A spot in the national championship game? Duke was there.

But could it stay there? That's generally what separated North Carolina from the rest of the Atlantic Coast Conference. Someone like N.C. State with Sidney Lowe and Thurl Bailey, or Georgia Tech with Mark Price and John Salley, would put together an abnormally strong recruiting class and make a run at the Tar Heels. After the run was complete and the recruiting class was gone, N.C. State or Georgia Tech or whomever would return to the middle of the ACC pack. There at the top would be North Carolina, a college basketball corporation, waiting for the next challenge.

Now, in 1986-87, it was Duke's turn to take another swipe at the king-of-the-hill Tar Heels. They would take it with their major artillery gone: Mark Alarie, Johnny Dawkins, Jay Bilas and David Henderson had graduated, leaving four holes in the starting lineup for Krzyzewski to fill. Point guard Tommy Amaker was back for his senior season. The rest of the lineup included Danny Ferry, now a sophomore and ready to prove his status as the top recruit in the country two years earlier, and Billy King, the defensive wizard whose every shot on offense was an adventure. Like Alarie and Dawkins three years earlier, Ferry spent the summer between his freshman and sophomore seasons expanding his game on the international stage, starting for the United States' team at the World University Games, which won the silver medal at Zagreb, Yugoslavia. Krzyzewski also planned to start forward John Smith, a sophomore whose game was about as creative as his name, and Kevin Strickland, a junior who had been a reserve for two seasons, at guard, opposite Amaker.

The rest of the basketball world was not impressed. Even though the ACC as a whole had taken a serious talent hit that year – along with Duke's four starters, Georgia Tech said good-bye to Price and Salley; North Carolina lost Brad Daugherty and Steve Hale; and Maryland lost ACC Player of the Year Len Bias – Duke's losses were thought to be the worst of the group. The Blue Devils were predicted to finish no higher than sixth of the eight teams that season in the ACC.

They finished third with a 9-5 mark in conference play, and won twenty-four games overall. It was the kind of season Dean Smith at North Carolina had made a career out of – lose a handful of stars, pull out another twenty wins anyhow, and move on. Unranked at the beginning of the year, Duke rose to No. 12 by midseason and finished the year ranked seventeenth. The season ended in the NCAA tournament's Sweet Sixteen with a six-point loss to No. 3 Indiana, coached by Krzyzewski's friend and mentor, Bobby Knight. The Hoosiers would go on to win the national championship. Krzyzewski and Duke would go on the following season to resume the early stages of the best nine-year run of any team this side of UCLA's 1960s and 1970s juggernaut.

It all began with a bus ride.

The 1987-88 Duke team wasn't so different from the previous season's group. Amaker was gone, but in his place was Quin Snyder, another cerebral point guard who, like Amaker, wasn't going to win games with his shooting but could make a difference as a playmaker on offense and a disruptive force on defense. Beyond that, three starters returned, including Ferry, who would emerge that season as the best forward in college basketball. In one game in 1988, Ferry scored fifty-eight points against Miami, ten more than the No. 2 single-game performance in Duke history, the forty-eight points Dick Groat hung on North Carolina in 1952.

Duke began the season ranked fifteenth but spent most of the year in the Top 10. The season, however, began to slip away from the Blue Devils in late February. Ranked fifth in the country, Duke lost by eleven points to No. 18 N.C. State, by four to No. 20 Georgia Tech, and then by two to an unranked Clemson team the Blue Devils had spanked 101-63 earlier in the season at Cameron Indoor Stadium. This time the game was played at Clemson, where Duke played probably its worst game of the season and then trudged outside to the bus, where Krzyzewski was waiting.

The players called what followed "The Great Meeting."

Krzyzewski wasn't screaming. He wasn't cursing. He just wanted to know what had happened to the team that had won eight of its first ten Atlantic Coast Conference games. After rising from his seat in the second row of the bus, Krzyzewski made his way to the back and asked a simple question: "What's wrong here?"

"There wasn't any yelling or anything," Krzyzewski said of the four-hour bus ride from Clemson to Durham. "It just seemed they had gotten to thinking more about improving their games than improving our game. They got away from the focus that if you reach team goals, you will reach individual goals."

What Krzyzewski learned was that his close-knit team had maybe let that closeness get in the way of the improvement that can come from brutal honesty.

"We're such good friends off the court that I think it hurt us on the court," said Kevin Strickland, a senior co-captain along with Billy King. "Quin (Snyder) or Billy would hesitate in using a harsh word when that's what was needed. We had to say, 'We're all men here, and if you can't take it, you shouldn't play.'"

The meeting served its purpose. Maybe too well. Said Strickland: "After the meeting, I was getting cussed out all the time."

Cussing works. The Blue Devils climbed off that bus in Durham, then climbed down No. 9 North Carolina's throat four days later, beating the Tar Heels 96-81 in the regular-season finale at Cameron Indoor Stadium, where King and Strickland played their final home games. Duke and North Carolina would run into each other again one week later in the ACC tournament championship game, with the same result. Duke won, and rode that momentum all the way to the Final Four. Along the way, the Blue Devils upset the No. 1 team in the country, Temple, 63-53 in the East regional title game at East Rutherford, New Jersey.

What, exactly, had Krzyzewski said on the bus after the Clemson game? Nothing terribly complicated. He merely pointed out that some of the players seemed to have forgotten what their roles were. Snyder (5.7 assists per game) ran the offense. King ran the defense. Ferry (19.1 points per game) and Strickland (16.3 points) were the shooters. Robert Brickey and King set screens. Everyone rebounded. Those were the roles.

"There were so many questions to be answered that season," Krzyzewski said. "Roles – big roles, such as Quin's – were uncertain. Some people had us rated highly, some didn't. I didn't know what the hell we were going to do. I just knew we weren't a great basketball team, but I thought we could be a real good basketball team that would get even better."

Former reserve Snyder emerged as a steady hand running the offense, an evolution that was painful at first. Snyder had barely played his first two seasons with the team, sitting on the bench behind Dawkins and Amaker. Thrust into the starting point guard position, the most demanding position to play for a former point guard like Krzyzewski, Snyder wobbled from the gate. He misread fast-break opportunities and threw balls away, sometimes into the crowd. By midseason he had settled into a nice groove, though, and Duke rode Snyder's leadership all the way to the 1988 Final Four.

The joy ride ended against Kansas, a 66-59 loss that capped a sorry weekend for Krzyzewski. While he was in Kansas City, Missouri, losing to the Jayhawks in front of a decidedly pro-Kansas crowd, his home was broken into in Durham and his car, a 1987 Chevrolet Celebrity, was stolen. The robber escaped with almost nothing because one of Krzyzewski's neighbors thwarted his getaway, chasing the stolen car to a dead end, where a man hopped out and ran for cover in the woods. Meanwhile, for the second consecutive season, the Blue Devils' year had ended against the team that would eventually win the national championship. Kansas would go on to defeat Oklahoma for the title.

Krzyzewski and Duke would get there soon enough.

First, though, Duke had to convince Krzyzewski not to go anywhere. It wasn't that difficult. One day after the season ended, UCLA approached Krzyzewski about becoming the Bruins' next coach. "They contacted me and expressed a sincere interest," he said, "but I just didn't have an interest. They have a great school and a great program, but I think we have that, too. I appreciated their interest, but I just (wasn't going) to talk to them."

Krzyzewski wasn't finished turning schools down.

National champion Kansas, the school that produced Dean Smith and saw its leader, Larry Brown, depart for the NBA, also made an inquiry into Krzyzewski's availability later that summer, and Krzyzewski told the Jayhawks he simply wasn't available. Kansas then turned to a Smith assistant at North Carolina, Roy Williams. Illinois also made a run at Krzyzewski, but that, too, was halted rather quickly. A few years later, when Notre Dame coach Digger Phelps was in the final season of his contract, Duke played the Fighting Irish at South Bend, Indiana, where the fans greeted Krzyzewski amorously: "Coach K, coach here. Coach K, coach here." Again, thanks – but no thanks.

"We have a great situation here at Duke," Krzyzewski said. "Why would I want to leave something this good?"

Indeed it was a good situation. It was going to get better, too.

By 1988-89 Duke was recognized as one of the premier programs in the country. No fluke, no one-year wonder in 1986, their twenty-four victories in 1987 and Final Four in 1988 solidified the Blue Devils' stature as a program with staying power. And the previous off-season, when three major basketball programs came calling, suggested Krzyzewski was as fine a coach as any. And of course there was this: Duke Athletic Director Tom Butters was no longer receiving bushels of mail calling for Krzyzewski's job.

Not with Danny Ferry back for his senior season. Snyder, too, was a senior and a co-captain with Ferry. In 1989, the Blue Devils started the season ranked No. 1 in the country and they held onto that spot until being demolished 91-71 by No. 13 North Carolina at Cameron Indoor Stadium, then losing three days later at unranked Wake Forest. Duke would finish the season ranked ninth but advance all the way to the Final Four – Krzyzewski's third in the past four seasons at Duke – where they lost to

Seton Hall. Ferry ended the season as the National Player of the Year for averaging 22.6 points, the most by one player at Duke since the 1960s, and 7.4 rebounds. And for a big guy, Ferry sure could shoot. He hit 42.5 percent of his three-pointers.

All of a sudden, Duke was a dynasty, or at least as close to a dynasty as you saw in college basketball in the late 1980s, what with players leaving early for the NBA, coaches skipping from one school to the next and the typical uncertainties of recruiting. What had happened in Durham? The players, for one thing. Thanks to success on the recruiting trail, Krzyzewski was no longer trying to win games with heady, if not terribly physically gifted, players like Tom Emma and Dan Meagher. His job on the court became significantly easier when he began looking around the huddle during time-outs and seeing the faces of Johnny Dawkins, Mark Alarie and David Henderson, or Danny Ferry, Tommy Amaker and Billy King. Recruiting was one answer. So, too, was the development of Krzyzewski as a coach. Shackled at Army by the physical limitations of his players, Krzyzewski found himself coaching some of the best athletes in the country at Duke, and his coaching style changed accordingly, particularly on offense. Krzyzewski wasn't afraid to do the unusual if he thought the unusual – not gimmicks, just something unusual – gave his team the best chance to win. That's why he wasn't afraid to let the biggest player on his early 1980s team, Mark Alarie, wander twenty feet from the basket to shoot a jumper, and it's also why in the late 1980s Krzyzewski let a 6-foot-5 jumping jack named Robert Brickey play center while the 6'10" Ferry roamed the perimeter.

"I think Mike started to expand himself as a coach after a few years at Duke," said Krzyzewski's longtime Army and Duke assistant, Pete Gaudet. "It's something you'd expect from a lot of coaches as they get more and more comfortable wherever they are, though I'm not saying you'd expect a lot of coaches to win like Mike did. His teams specialize in defense, no question about it, but to underestimate Mike as an offensive coach would be a big, big mistake."

To underestimate the power of Krzyzewski's assistant coaches at Duke, and their role in the Blue Devils' evolution from mediocrity to national powerhouse, also would be a mistake, former Duke forward and co-captain Kenny Dennard believes. Krzyzewski began hiring assistants like Bob Bender and Mike Brey. Bender was a former transfer from Indiana who came to Duke in 1978 and, after biding his time for several years as a businessman in Durham, was added to Krzyzewski's staff in 1984. Brey coached under the renowned Morgan Wootten at DeMatha High in Washington D.C., and served as the go-between for every college recruiting Danny Ferry in 1985. Krzyzewski came away impressed with Brey as a person and a basketball coach, and when his staff had an opening in 1988, Krzyzewski filled it with Brey. In 1989, Krzyzewski added his former point guard, Tommy Amaker, to the staff.

"Mike had a different philosophy about his staff as the years went on at Duke," Dennard said. "His early staffs were not to the quality of the later guys, the guys who helped bring Duke to the forefront of college basketball. Look what Bob Bender did, Mike Brey, Tommy Amaker. It's not just the head coach. It's the assistants too, and Coach K really refined his staff and had a very good staffing philosophy.

"Look, when he got there his staff was not at the level he wanted it to be. I mean nothing personal against the guys who were there. Chuck Swenson is a great guy, but he's not a Tom Amaker. When (Krzyzewski) brought in Bob Bender and got Pete Gaudet, that's when you saw the program come into its own. You can measure the recruiting. What you can't measure is the bench coaching, which you know was elevated by the great groups they had in the 1980s. What Mike did with his staff was as important as what he did on the floor."

In 1999 Bender was the coach at Washington and Brey was the coach at Delaware, two programs that were making appearances in the NCAA tournament, and both were being mentioned prominently for openings at major schools across the country. Krzyzewski also added Gaudet in 1984, bringing his former assistant at Army to the ACC after Gaudet served as Krzyzewski's replacement with the Cadets for two seasons. Gaudet gave Krzyzewski's ever-changing staff consistency as Swenson left in 1987 for William & Mary, Bender left for Washington and Brey readied to leave for Delaware in 1995.

"I didn't go out on the road and recruit," Gaudet said. "That was something Mike and I talked about and decided it would be best. He wanted stability in that third (assistant) position. Guys like Swenson and Bender and Brey, when they did well recruiting, he knew they would get looks at other jobs. He wanted some continuity, and I was it."

Gaudet would move on one day, too. That wasn't a pretty situation. More on that later.

———

The 1989 season also saw the introduction of a player Krzyzewski had fervently recruited the season before, a player who would become perhaps the biggest enigma ever to play at Duke. Certainly, freshman Christian Laettner was the most ticklish personality in Durham since the neurotic Art Heyman in the mid-1960s. Krzyzewski envisioned Laettner, a 6-foot-10 power forward from Angola, New York, along the same lines as Danny Ferry, the reigning National Player of the Year with the feathery shooting touch to go with the power forward's body.

Laettner, though, wasn't as interested in Duke as Duke was in him. He was hoping to sign with North Carolina and play for Dean Smith, but was stung when Smith told him the Tar Heels wanted to sign only one power forward, and that the No. 1 power forward on their list was an in-state player named Kenny Williams. Smith came back to Laettner a short time later, after it had become apparent that Williams was going to struggle to qualify academically, but by then it was too late. Christian Laettner was Duke property.

Heaven help everyone involved.

"He was stubborn, he had a strong personality, he was tough. He could be a little too tough, I guess some of his teammates would say," said Gaudet, whose job for all of Laettner's four years at Duke was to work with the Blue Devils' big men. "But I thought he was wonderful. For the small amount of stuff you might have to deal with, with Christian, he was still wonderful to work with."

And wonderful to play with, as long as winning was all that mattered. If making nice in practice, being friends off the court, and hanging out on Thursday nights was what a player wanted, then Laettner was the wrong guy to see. But if winning was the goal, why, no one won like Laettner. He played in the Final Four all four seasons at Duke, reached the national championship game the last three years, and won the title the last two. "Christian was a big-time winner," said Marty Clark, a Duke guard from 1991-94 who was a freshman on Laettner's final Duke team.

But there were ... issues. Laettner refused to let up on his teammates, especially the younger ones, and it didn't matter if it was late March and the Final Four was approaching or early June and some guys were merely playing a pick-up game inside Cameron. In one pickup game the summer before his senior season, Laettner shoved teammate Grant Hill, only a freshman but already considered among the greatest athletes ever to play for Duke, and certainly the best to play for Krzyzewski. Hill landed on the floor with a crack, his wrist hurt, and he walked off the court for a breather. Unsatisfied, Laettner walked over to Hill on the sideline and accused him of faking the injury. For punctuation, Laettner gave Hill a shove. Hill returned to the court. Laettner had won.

During his senior season Laettner practically adopted Cherokee Parks, the freshman power forward whom Krzyzewski was grooming as Laettner's replacement the following year. Being adopted by Laettner probably made the 6-foot-11 Parks a better player. It definitely made him unhappy. "You get to the point where you don't want to be around the guy at all," Parks once said of Laettner. "He was always pissing me off. Maybe he was trying to make me better. Maybe he just liked pissing me off. I never asked."

Parks, whose parents were into the earthiness of the 1960s – hence his first name – wasn't into negativity. Some days he was in the locker room earlier than he should have been, simply to get away from Laettner, whose idea of adopting a younger teammate meant banging on him physically and abusing him verbally. Krzyzewski saw what was happening, and, for the most part, let it be. He knew Laettner was the kind of leader who tried to mold his younger teammates through fire, and he also knew Parks was the type player who could use that sort of molding. Parks rarely volunteered to stay late after practice, as did so many of his teammates.

"I remember with about a month left in the (1991-92) season, people said stuff about Christian and Cherokee not getting along," Gaudet said. "I remember one time Christian said something to me because Cherokee was leaving practice when it was over, not staying for extra shooting like some other guys did. Whether this was Christian being a smart guy or whatever I don't know, but he said, 'Coach, can we have somebody stay at practice to put a hand in my face on my jumper?' So I'm like, 'Cherokee, get over here,' and for a month we did jumpers with a hand in his face. Along with Christian getting extra practice in game-type situations, what that also meant was Chief (Parks) had to stay around. I know it made

Parks a better player."

It wasn't like Krzyzewski gave Laettner carte blanche to do as he pleased. By his senior season Laettner was the best player in the country, and no one in the country knew that better than Laettner himself. When Duke played at Boston University that season, the overmatched, under-sized Terriers played Laettner the only way they knew how – they fouled him repeatedly. Laettner began to get angered by the tactic, tossing snide looks at the Boston players and making eyes at the referees as well. Krzyzewski saw what was happening and said to his star forward, "So, you think you're too good to get fouled?"

A year earlier, Laettner ran amok in a 22-point loss to North Carolina in the Atlantic Coast Conference tourna-ment, yelling at teammates, cursing in general, loud enough for people courtside to hear. It wasn't enough for Krzyzewski to tell Laettner that his act was getting old. Krzyzewski *showed* him. He had Gaudet piece together a three-minute tape of Laettner in the North Carolina game, and sat Laettner down privately for a screening in the days leading up to the NCAA tournament. "You look," Krzyzewski told Laettner, as reported in *A Season is a Lifetime*. "The yelling, this whole thing. You were bad, Christian, and that bothers me because you're not bad, you're a hell of a player, but if you do that in the (NCAA) tournament, you're not going to play."

Krzyzewski then trained his eyes on Laettner's and said, "If you don't believe that, test me."

Laettner kept his eyes where they were and said, "It will never happen again."

But it did, of course. In a 72-68 loss to Wake Forest the next season, Laettner was called for two technical fouls, the first for complaining about a referee's call, the second for hanging on the rim after a dunk. Laettner had a chance to atone for his technicals when Duke trailed 70-68 with five seconds to play and Krzyzewski called for Grant Hill to throw an inbounds pass to Laettner, who would try to create something to tie the game. Laettner caught Hill's pass near midcourt, but his foot was on the boundary, and the referees gave the ball to Wake Forest. Game over.

The next day, in front of the entire team, Krzyzewski reminded his superstar who was the boss of Duke basketball. And it wasn't the superstar.

"Last year," he began with Laettner, "when you were hungry and had something to prove, you did the job. You were terrific. Now you think you're a hot ticket. Well, you suck. You absolutely suck."

The next week would be the season finale, Laettner's last game at Cameron Indoor Stadium. On top of that, Laettner had already been told his number would be retired in a ceremony before that game. Now, Krzyzewski was having second thoughts. And, according to *A Season is a Lifetime*, he let Laettner know about those second thoughts. "A big part of me doesn't even want to start you," he told Laettner. "That's the position you placed me in. If your uniform wasn't being retired, you wouldn't start."

Fired up, Laettner went out the next day in practice and threw the 245-pound Parks aside while going for a rebound. Parks landed on Hill, who had to be taken to Duke Hospital for tests on his twisted ankle. No one was angry with Laettner. He was just playing aggressively, as Krzyzewski had challenged him to do the previous day in front of the whole team. And as far as Gaudet was concerned, Laettner was great to work with on a day-to-day basis.

"Knowing other kids, I would not say Christian was high maintenance," Gaudet said. "If people ask me who was the best player you ever ended up coaching, because I ended up drifting with the big guys, well, Danny Ferry was terrific, Mark Alarie had an unbelievable work ethic and was the most efficient player we had, but Laettner worked on his game as much as anyone and he was intense. He was great."

On one of Laettner's first days at Duke, Gaudet thought he and Laettner were going to have a problem. "I remember telling him something about catching the ball and doing this footwork at the foul line, and he gave me a real odd look, a challenging look. I ignored it," Gaudet said. "We did the same play again, and he kind of gave me the same look. I was a little defensive and kind of went after him: 'Look, Christian, what's the problem with this?'"

"He just said, 'I don't know, I'm an idiot, I just can't do it.' He was mad at himself. I was thinking the look was at me, but it was at himself. He was unhappy with himself. I backed off and said, 'Wow, this guy's going to be good.'"

That he was. Laettner started at center as a freshman because he was too good not to start, and because center was the only position available. He averaged 8.9 points a game that season, taking – and making – only one three-pointer all year. By the end of his career, Laettner had transformed himself, much like Alarie several years earlier, into a deadly long-range shooter. No Duke player has ever shot as well from three-point range in one season as Laettner did as a senior, when he hit 55.7 percent of his bombs. That season he averaged 21.5 points and 7.9 rebounds a game and was the National Player of the Year.

"Christian Laettner," Krzyzewski said, "could flat-out play."

Duke didn't live by Laettner alone. The next season, 1989-90, a freshman point guard named Bobby Hurley joined the Blue Devils and immediately began embarking on a record-setting career he would finish as the NCAA's all-time leader in assists with 1,076. Hurley's first assist came with nearly ten minutes to play in the first half of his first collegiate game, against Harvard, and the recipient was backcourt mate Billy McCaffrey, who would later transfer because he, too, wanted to play point guard and that position belonged to Hurley. Four years later,

Hurley broke the NCAA assist record on a feed to center Eric Meek, replacing another Atlantic Coast Conference and local point guard, N.C. State's Chris Corchiani, who had racked up 1,038 assists from 1987 to 1991 in Raleigh.

Like Laettner, Hurley didn't exactly want to play for Duke in the beginning, either. In high school Hurley played for his father, legendary New Jersey private school coach Bob Hurley, and in college he wanted to play for another legend – Dean Smith at North Carolina. But Smith hadn't learned his lesson from the Kenny Williams recruiting fiasco that cost him a shot at Laettner in the previous year's recruiting class. Smith assumed the Tar Heels were going to get New York City star point guard Kenny Anderson, who played at the same high school that had produced another former North Carolina point guard named Kenny, Kenny Smith, and who, since his sophomore season of high school, had made rumblings about playing his collegiate ball in Chapel Hill. Smith took those rumblings literally. Anderson did not. When he chose to play at Georgia Tech instead, Anderson commented that he didn't want to be "another horse in Dean Smith's stable." Hurley, the place horse in Smith's point guard derby, decided he'd rather be the No. 1 option at Duke than the No. 2 choice at North Carolina, so he signed with Krzyzewski.

Of all the great point guards Krzyzewski has had – Johnny Dawkins for one season, then Tommy Amaker for four, then Quin Snyder, and later Steve Wojciechowski and William Avery – Hurley was, statistically, the best of them all. Nobody created opportunities for his teammates like Hurley, obviously, given his NCAA assist record, but it was more than that. Hurley also was an underrated scorer, averaging more points a game in one season – an even seventeen per game as a senior – than any of the other pure point guards to play for Krzyzewski. Dawkins averaged 18.1 points in his lone season at the point, but he was a shooting guard playing the point position, and averaged only 4.1 assists that year.

What drove Hurley, a 6-foot, 165-pound, hollow-eyed ghost of a point guard, to greatness was his competitive spirit. He was a nuisance on defense who began covering the other team's point guard almost as soon as that unfortunate soul received the inbounds pass, as much as ninety feet away from his basket, and hounded him all the way up the court. Jay Bilas, the former Duke center who spent two seasons as a Krzyzewski assistant coach during the Hurley era, remembers almost feeling sorry for the other team's point guard. "Bobby was just all over whoever he was guarding, and it lasted for forty minutes," Bilas said. "And the thing was, Bobby never seemed to get tired. Imagine how debilitating that must be for the other guy if you see Bobby Hurley in your face all game, and you're breathing hard, grabbing your shorts, and (Hurley) seems like he could go another forty minutes. It was crazy."

No, it was Hurley. He even managed to turn the weight room into a place for competition. Hurley wasn't too keen on the StairMaster workout machine, but one day he noticed that Bilas – a StairMaster regular – owned the Duke record of 759 floors in one workout. One day Bilas came into the weight room for his daily date with the StairMaster, and found a note taped to the machine by Hurley – "800 floors. Top that, Bilas." (And Bilas did, eventually upping the record to 856 floors, a score Hurley conceded was the record.)

The strong-willed Laettner and the equally stubborn Hurley clashed over and over, especially during Hurley's freshman season, their feud finally getting to the point where Hurley stopped in Krzyzewski's office one day after practice and issued a formal complaint. "Tell Christian to quit getting on me all the time," Hurley said, as reported in *A Season is a Lifetime*. "I don't deserve it."

Krzyzewski, sensing a moment that could make or break the chemistry of this team and teams to come, answered: "Tell him yourself." Hurley did take care of the matter himself, confronting Laettner one day in the locker room, his bold act actually impressing Laettner, earning his respect.

————

Hurley's legendary competitiveness may have hurt the Blue Devils that first season, in 1989-90, but only in the final game of the year – the national championship game against UNLV, the second for Duke under Krzyzewski. To get there, Duke had to overcome a dismal stretch that began in late February when it lost four of six games, including two losses to unranked local foes N.C. State and North Carolina. The latter was a twelve-point blowout in the final game at Cameron Indoor Stadium for three Duke senior starters: Robert Brickey, Alaa Abdelnaby and Phil Henderson. For reasons ranging from effort on the court to effort in the classroom, it was a senior class that never seemed to capture the fancy of Krzyzewski, who named only one of the three seniors, Brickey, a team captain. On the heels of that dismal end to the regular season, the Blue Devils definitely didn't seem ready for a run at their third consecutive Final Four a week later when they lost by eleven points in the second round of the Atlantic Coast Conference tournament at Charlotte.

But Duke got hot again at the right time – NCAA tournament time – and with some tomfoolery from Laettner and Krzyzewski, the Blue Devils eked into the Final Four. The place was the Meadowlands at East Rutherford, New Jersey, where they had defeated No. 1 Temple two years earlier. Just as it had been in 1988, this was the East regional championship game against a No. 1 seed – Connecticut – only this time Duke trailed 78-77 in the final seconds of overtime. Duke had the ball, and Krzyzewski called a play for Laettner to find Henderson with the inbounds pass, and for Henderson to come off a screen and take the shot. But when both teams set up for the inbounds play and

Krzyzewski saw the Huskies had chosen to leave Laettner, the inbounds passer, alone, Krzyzewski made an audible. He told Laettner to hit Brian Davis with the pass and get the ball back as soon as he could, and to take the open jump shot that would be there. Laettner did as he was told, sank the double-pumping, leaning eighteen-footer, and Duke won 79-78.

Later, Connecticut coach Jim Calhoun would essentially admit to having been outfoxed on the play. Calhoun, who normally attended every Final Four as a spectator, couldn't bring himself to attend the 1990 game at Denver. "There were two names I just didn't want to hear," Calhoun said nine years later. "One was Christian Laettner. The other was Mike Krzyzewski."

Duke bludgeoned Arkansas 97-83 in the national semifinals, freezing the Razorbacks' famed "forty minutes of hell" defense with an efficient offense that got a combined eighty-six points from Brickey, Laettner, Abdelnaby and Henderson. That set up the national title meeting with the University of Nevada-Las Vegas, ranked second in the country and featuring a lineup of future NBA players Larry Johnson, Stacey Augmon, Anderson Hunt and Greg Anthony. Meanwhile, there was trouble in the Duke camp. Hurley, the freshman point guard whose leadership on offense would be critical against the Runnin Rebels' "amoeba" defense, had come down with a stomach virus. He spent most of the day Sunday, twenty-four hours before the game, in bed. With Hurley out anyway, Krzyzewski called off practice that day to let the rest of the team rest, too.

All that did was give the national media on hand an entire day to think up the right storyline for the Duke-UNLV matchup, Good vs. Evil. It was an easy and perhaps borderline racist title for the game, pitting Duke with its lily-white image – not to mention white stars like Laettner and Hurley – against UNLV with its renegade coach, Jerry Tarkanian, and an all-black lineup. There was no animosity on either side, though. Tarkanian even went so far as to send Krzyzewski a note, a few years earlier, letting the Duke coach know how impressed he was with the way the Blue Devils went about the business of winning. For his part, Krzyzewski did his part to silence the Good and Evil talk.

"I don't look at it that way," Krzyzewski said. "I really respect them as a basketball team and as people. I know a couple of their players and hope they end up playing for me this summer (in the 1990 World Championships). Geez, I've ridiculed the press and charged officials. We've yelled at one another. We've been pretty bad, too, I think."

UNLV point guard Greg Anthony fought the Good vs. Evil typecast with humor, razzing the media by asking, "What, are you labeling Duke the bad boys?" Tarkanian, meanwhile, backed off the image of his having an outcast team living in Sin City. "I never gamble at all," Tarkanian said. "I've never played a slot machine in my life. We live a totally different life than people perceive."

Bobby Hurley didn't care about any of that. He spent the night before the title game running to and from the bathroom of his hotel room, and then spent most of the hours leading up to the game Monday night the same way. Hurley still was battling an acute case of diarrhea by the time the game rolled around, but he insisted on playing as much as he could. Although Duke had other options at point guard – namely, Billy McCaffrey – Krzyzewski let Hurley play through his problems, which were so bad that the national television cameras often caught him sprinting away from the Duke bench and into the locker room, then returning a few minutes later and re-entering the game. Hurley finished the game with his worst stats of the season – two points, three assists – and Duke lost 103-73.

Revenge would come soon. And it would be sweet.

Under Krzyzewski, the coach Duke boosters had

wanted fired less than ten years earlier, the Blue Devils were doing things teams just didn't do. Three straight Final Fours? Consecutive season victory totals of twenty-eight, twenty-eight and twenty-nine? It just wasn't done. But still, something was missing. A national championship. And someone was missing.

His name was Grant Hill.

Krzyzewski added the final piece to his royal blue puzzle that year, signing the 6-foot-8 Hill from Reston, Virginia. And, as was the case with Laettner and Hurley, Krzyzewski's gain was Dean Smith's loss. Unlike Laettner and Hurley, who were secondary choices for the Tar Heels and decided to go elsewhere, Grant Hill was a primary target for Smith. Smith liked everything about Hill, and not just his fluid athletic ability and the way he played point guard in high school despite usually being the tallest player on the court.

Smith was intrigued by Hill's background. The son of former Yale and Dallas Cowboys running back Calvin Hill, Grant actually was named by a teammate of his father, Dallas quarterback Roger Staubach. Grant Hill's mother Janet also had an interesting tale to tell, though hers would come one year later when her former roommate at Wellesley, Hillary Rodham Clinton, became the First Lady. Despite those strong Democratic ties, erstwhile Republican Krzyzewski was more than willing to have Hill play on his team.

Dean Smith thought he was going to get Hill, especially when Calvin sidled up to him one day and told the North Carolina coach how much he – Calvin – liked the Tar Heels. His son also liked the Tar Heels. "All my life," Grant Hill said. "As far back as I can remember. I started loving the game of basketball after watching the Tar Heels win the national championship (in 1982)."

Krzyzewski lurked in the background. He made his visit to Hill's house memorable, but not suffocating. The same goes for the way Duke recruited Hill. Quality, not quantity, time was spent. "They didn't bother me," Hill said of the Blue Devils. "Other schools were all over me. I got calls all the time. All the time. Duke called once a week. I appreciated that."

The makeup of Krzyzewski's staff didn't hurt. Amaker, the assistant and former point guard, also was from Northern Virginia. Mike Brey, another assistant, came from a Washington D.C. area powerhouse, DeMatha, that the Hills knew all about. Eventually Hill chose Duke. "I shocked my parents and everyone else. I know I shocked Duke," he said. "I think they thought I was going to Carolina."

Hill went to Duke, and so did the missing jewel in Krzyzewski's crown – the national championship. In Hill's first year, the 1990-91 season, the Blue Devils weren't thought to be as strong as they had been two years earlier. Duke had opened the 1988-89 season with senior, Danny Ferry, as the preseason No. 1 team in the country. Two years later, even though Laettner and Hurley were back, Duke had lost three senior starters and was picked sixth nationally. By early January, the Blue Devils had dropped to fourteenth, even though their only three losses were to ranked teams. No. 2 Arkansas on a neutral floor, No. 6 Georgetown at Landover, Maryland, and No. 18 Virginia at Charlottesville, Virginia. Duke would lose to North Carolina in the ACC tournament, and then it wouldn't lose again until the next season.

The North Carolina loss was the one where, afterward, Krzyzewski called Laettner into his office and dared him to act that poorly again. Krzyzewski and Laettner would have an even more bizarre – but shorter and infinitely happier – conversation a few weeks later. First, though, Duke had to get past the team that had humbled it the year before, Nevada-Las Vegas, in the Final Four. The last time Duke had played the Runnin' Rebels, Bobby Hurley was seen sprinting for the locker room, overcome with diarrhea. This time Hurley was healthy, and UNLV wasn't ready. Entering the Final Four, UNLV was two victories away from capping an unbeaten season and entering the ranks of the great teams of all time, a short list that included Indiana in 1976, N.C. State in 1974, UCLA in the late 1960s with Lew Alcindor and early 1970s with Bill Walton, and a handful of others. UNLV returned all of its stars from the 1990 national championship squad that had dismantled Duke 103-73, but Duke had star power of its own: Laettner, Grant Hill, an emerging Brian Davis. And Hurley. Don't forget Hurley. A year after posting two points and three assists against UNLV, Hurley produced twelve points and seven assists in the 1991 Final Four.

The game came down to this: tie score, 77-all, 12.7 seconds left, Christian Laettner standing at the foul line with two free throws. In the huddle before the foul shots, Krzyzewski and Laettner had their conversation. Krzyzewski looked at Laettner, grinned, and asked, "You all right?" Laettner grinned back and nodded his head. Inside joke. Two years earlier, after the loss to Seton Hall in the Final Four, Krzyzewski couldn't get through the post-game locker room scene without crying for his senior co-captains, Danny Ferry and Quin Snyder, who would graduate without a national title. Stunned by the display of naked emotion from his coach, Laettner later that night visited Krzyzewski in his hotel room and asked, over and over, "You all right?"

Two years later, Krzyzewski was all right, Laettner was all right, the two free throws were all right, and Duke beat the latest "greatest team of all time," 79-77.

And then, maybe, Duke got cocky. Kansas awaited in the national championship game, and the No. 12-ranked Jayhawks were no UNLV. Danny Manning was long gone from the Kansas roster, leaving behind a point guard with a great name – Adonis Jordan – and a supporting cast of no-names. The day after the UNLV game, and the day before Kansas, Duke players arrived at the dome in Indianapolis with an air of invincibility. Krzyzewski didn't like it. Two of his players were wearing Indiana Jones-style hats. The rest were swaggering around the locker room. Krzyzewski let them have it.

"I don't like the way you're walking, talking, anything," Krzyzewski said, as reported in *A Season is a Lifetime*. "You should go watch Vegas tapes because there's no way you can beat Kansas. Go back to the hotel and let the fans kiss your ass."

Krzyzewski sent his team out and canceled practice, but after about five minutes the players remained on the court, ready to practice. Krzyzewski could see the change. They were ready. "We're national champs as long as you keep this focus," he told them.

Twenty-four hours later, they were. Duke beat Kansas 72-65, and Krzyzewski had his first national championship. Hill, the freshman who had been named by Dallas Cowboys quarterback Roger Staubach, showed off his hands – and his springs – early in the game, soaring over the rim to catch Hurley's alley-oop pass and hurling it through the rim, sucking the noise for an instant completely out of the domed stadium. Greg Koubek, a senior and co-captain, scored Duke's first five points, and though he wouldn't score again, they were an emotional lift for Duke and a dagger into the heart of Kansas. Laettner, who had eighteen points and ten rebounds in the title game, was named Most Valuable Player of the Final Four. He was joined on the All-Final Four team by Hurley and reserve guard Billy McCaffrey, who had sixteen points against Kansas.

Up in the stands, a group of Krzyzewski's childhood friends sat and watched it unfold. Larry Kusch – 'Twams' to his friends from the north side of Chicago – sent Krzyzewski a note as the Duke coach and his team celebrated on the court. Somehow the note made its way to Krzyzewski's hands, right there on the court. "Congratulations," it said. It was signed: "Columbos forever."

Krzyzewski read the note and thought: "Can we do this again? I'd really like to do this again."

Good idea, Mickey.

There was something of an icky beginning to Duke's title defense – oops, wrong word. Defense. Krzyzewski didn't want to call it that. He refused, as a matter of fact. On the first day of practice for the 1991-92 season, Krzyzewski told his players they would not be defending the national championship. Defending? Too passive. No, the Blue Devils, Krzyzewski told them, would pursue the 1992 national championship – looking ahead to where they wanted to go, not backward at where they already had been.

But the start to this pursuit of a second consecutive national championship wasn't as smooth as Krzyzewski would have liked. Billy McCaffrey, the explosive guard who chafed at his backup point guard/shooting guard role, announced he wasn't coming back for his junior season. At the urging of his father, McCaffrey had decided to transfer to Vanderbilt. The departure of McCaffrey, who was named to the All-Final Four team the previous season, was so unexpected that it surprised even his roommate, Bobby Hurley, the player who had the starting point guard job McCaffrey so badly coveted. This was no small loss. McCaffrey had been one of the country's top recruits two years earlier, a gym rat who could do wondrous things with the basketball. Years later, former Duke star Danny Ferry, by then with the NBA's Cleveland Cavaliers, would complain to former Duke assistant Pete Gaudet that McCaffrey, an NBA teammate in Cleveland, shot too much. "Well," Gaudet counseled Ferry, "why don't you tell him to stop shooting so much?"

Ferry's response: "What can I do? He makes all his shots."

That's how good McCaffrey was. But this is how good

Duke was in that 1991-92 season: The Blue Devils did not miss him at all. They returned every starter but Koubek, the senior forward, and in his place was the more talented Brian Davis. The other four starters: Laettner, Grant Hill, Thomas Hill, Hurley. The bench included future NBA lottery pick Cherokee Parks, a freshman on that team. Duke started the regular season ranked No. 1 in the country and Duke ended the regular season ranked No. 1 in the country, and it stayed there every week in between, too. Not even losses to North Carolina, by two in the Smith Center, and to Wake Forest, by four at Winston-Salem, could knock the Blue Devils out of the No. 1 spot for even a week.

It was a fun year. It was the season Hurley, a junior, would break Tommy Amaker's Duke record for career assists. On February 1 of that season, against Notre Dame, Hurley quickly passed out seven assists to move within one assist of Amaker's school record of 708. Amaker, by now Krzyzewski's top assistant, looked over at the head coach and said, "Hurley's dragging. Better get him out." Knowing what Amaker was doing but liking it, Krzyzewski agreed, and for Hurley the record assist had to wait one more game. It didn't hurt matters that the record-tying and record-breaking assists came in that next game – against North Carolina.

It was a trying year, too. It seems Duke might have become too good, too perfect. Two years earlier, the Duke-UNLV championship game was dubbed Good vs. Evil. That was a compliment to Duke. Two years later, that was no longer a compliment. Duke had become too good, too perfect. Too arrogant? Too squeaky clean? That was the complaint heard inside and outside the state. According to Charles Pierce, a freelance magazine writer, "(UNLV's) Larry Johnson has more personality in his little finger than the five Duke starters."

Pierce went on to write, in a column for *The Basketball Times*, that, "You can't like this team simply for the way it plays. You have to like this team because it makes you feel so good about yourself – so righteous, so fundamentally superior, so clean that you squeak, a ghastly form of moral fascism that allows no one else to establish standards independently of your own because your privileges allow you to remain safe from your own failings."

Issues came up that season that simply do not come up in college basketball. Was Christian Laettner gay? That was how many interpreted some of his comments about his best friend and roommate, Brian Davis, about whom Laettner had said, "I just want to be with Brian." The rumors persisted for months until the NCAA tournament, when a writer from another state came right out and asked Laettner if he was gay.

No, Laettner said.

"Why didn't you say so before now?" the writer asked.

"Because no one asked me," Laettner said.

There you go. Laettner wasn't gay, and Duke wasn't going to be beaten again after February 23. The Blue Devils ripped through the ACC tournament, beating North Carolina by twenty in the title game, and then marched into the East regional championship game against Kentucky in Philadelphia, where the teams staged what some observers felt was the best college basketball game ever played. It might just have been the best individual game ever played, that individual being Duke's Christian Laettner.

You could make the argument for both cases. It went into overtime, and the lead changed hands five times in the final 31.5 seconds. First it was Laettner, bulling his way through a double-team and using the glass to sink a short shot. Duke 100-98. Then it was Jamal Mashburn, driving for a layup, being fouled by Antonio Lang and making the free throw for a three-point play with nineteen seconds left. Kentucky 101-100. Then it was Laettner, beating Mashburn on the other end and drawing Mashburn's fifth foul, then sinking both free throws with fourteen seconds left. Duke 102-101. Then it was Sean Woods, driving into the lane and banking a jumper over Laettner and high off the glass with 2.1 seconds left. Kentucky 103-102.

Timeout, Duke. In the huddle, Krzyzewski dropped his clipboard and began asking his players questions. He asked Grant Hill if he could make a three-quarter-court pass to Laettner at the opposite foul line. Yes, Hill said. Krzyzewski asked Laettner if he could catch it. Yes, Laettner said. If everything worked perfectly, Laettner still would have to get the ball into a shooting position, spin against one or two Kentucky defenders, and launch a jumper with a hand in his face. And make it. Or the season, and his career, would be over. Yes, Laettner said. He could do it.

On the periphery of the huddle was Duke assistant Pete Gaudet, remembering the days of January and February when Laettner had insisted that the 6-foot-11 freshman, Cherokee Parks, stay late after practice to put a hand in his face on outside jumpers.

"For a month we did jumpers with a hand in his face," Gaudet said. "I didn't think much of it, but all of a sudden, the season goes on, we keep playing, and lo and behold, Laettner has to hit a jumper with a hand in his face in the biggest game of the year."

He hit it, of course. With Kentucky's 6-foot-6 Deron Feldhaus on one side and 6'8" John Pelphrey on the other, Laettner caught the pass from Hill, faked right, spun left and drilled the seventeen-footer over Feldhaus.

"One of the most memorable shots in college basketball," Gaudet said. "People say that was a lucky shot, lucky shot. I remember thinking maybe, just maybe, there was a little something to that – where he demanded something more in a drill, and it paid off in the biggest way."

Laettner had taken twenty shots – ten from the floor, including one three-pointer, and ten more from the foul line – and hit them all for thirty-one points. A great game in a great game. And still there were two more games to play. Duke rallied from a twelve-point first-half deficit in the national semifinals against No. 5 Indiana and won 81-78 thanks to a late technical foul called against Krzyzewski's former coach at Army, Bobby Knight. Basically that was the national championship game, because in the real title game, Duke obliterated a young and No. 15-ranked Michigan team 71-51 to finish 34-2. Michigan had the "Fab Five" freshman class, but Duke had Laettner, Hurley, Grant Hill and company. Duke almost even had the most fabulous of the Fab Five, 6-foot-10 forward Chris Webber, who chose Michigan over Duke.

"How good would we have been with Webber?" Krzyzewski asked later.

Who knows? Who cares? Duke was, once again, the national champ.

———

Chapter Seven

AND THEN, THE CRASH

They called him "Mole Man." They called him that out of love, and they called him that out of frustration. Even when he was at home for the Christmas holidays, Mike Krzyzewski immersed himself in his Duke basketball team. While his family hustled and bustled around him, Krzyzewski hunkered down in front of the television in the living room and watched film of the Blue Devils' games. Hours and hours of film. He was the Mole Man.

This gave the family an idea. Maybe, and this is hindsight talking, maybe it should have given them a scare. Back in 1991, though, there were no worries. Duke was unstoppable, the very definition of a dynasty, and Krzyzewski was the ringmaster, watching game film at home during the Christmas holidays because that's what you do when you're the ringmaster of a dynasty. And so for Christmas 1991 his family bought him a gift that would help him watch the film and also give some relief to his occasionally testy back.

A massage chair.

However, the problems he would have were too big for any massage chair. Krzyzewski had no way of knowing it, but he was about to embark on a journey in which his back would give out on him, followed by the rest of his overextended body. "We kept winning, and I stayed right on top of it," he said. "That's not necessarily always fun. I don't know if I was ever completely one-dimensional, but I was totally focused during that period (from 1986-92). I was hard-driving."

The crash would come soon enough, and it would be spectacular. After the back-to-back national championships, the attention became suffocating. Most days that summer, scores of people lined the skinny hallway inside Cameron Indoor Stadium that led to the basketball offices. Krzyzewski vowed to sign every autograph, and Duke fans were dead set on seeing he lived up to that. The ones who didn't show up in person sent their memorabilia through the mail. Soon, two entire rooms in the athletic department were full of nothing but stuff for Krzyzewski and company to sign: shirts, hats, Final Four programs, basketballs. Lots and lots of basketballs. So many basketballs, Duke officials took every ball rack the school had out of storage for the summer and brought them into the offices, and soon a ball waiting to be signed filled every space on every rack. One day the people at Duke decided to move the balls down the hall from the basketball offices to a large meeting area called the Hall of Fame room, so student volunteers rolled the balls, station to station, down the hall. Basketball, meet boccie. Boxes of mail came into the office every day, and Krzyzewski signed every letter in response. The Duke players also were dragged into this mess, sitting for hours, two players to a table, autographing until their hands hurt.

It was madness, but it was madness for the right reasons, happy reasons, and Krzyzewski did his best to keep up. He also invited some of the madness. He served as an assistant to Chuck Daly – once a Duke assistant under Vic Bubas from 1964 to 1969 – on the 1992 U.S. Olympic basketball team, the original "Dream Team" of Michael Jordan and Magic Johnson, essentially going from the Final Four to training camp to Barcelona, Spain, to the gold medal presentation ceremony. It was a blast while it lasted. "What a fabulous four or five months it's been," Krzyzewski said that August. "It's just a continuation of the high from April."

The 1992-93 season offered a brief respite as the Blue Devils, with National Player of the Year Christian Laettner gone, along with starting forward Brian Davis, failed to reach the Final Four for the first time in six years, breaking the longest such streak since John Wooden's UCLA teams a quarter-century earlier. The 1993 Blue Devils finished 24-8 after fizzling down the stretch, losing their season finale by fourteen to North Carolina, then losing in the first round of the Atlantic Coast Conference tournament to Georgia Tech, then losing in the second round of the NCAA tournament to California. Duke's loss was North Carolina's gain. The Tar Heels, led by Eric Montross and George Lynch, won the national title – the second for Dean Smith, matching Krzyzewski's career total.

The frenzy around the Duke program had barely been quelled when the Blue Devils did it again, riding the senior leadership and playmaking of Grant Hill, a first-team All-American, to the Final Four and a spot in the 1994 national title game. There, Duke fell victim to a three-pointer by Arkansas' Scotty Thurman in the final minute that allowed the favored Razorbacks to escape with a 76-72 victory. Given the talent on that Duke team, especially compared to the past eight years, the 1994 season probably was one of Krzyzewski's best coaching jobs. It was Duke's seventh Final Four in nine years since the glorious class of Mark Alarie, Johnny Dawkins, Jay Bilas and David Henderson had begun it all in 1986.

It was, for Krzyzewski, the straw that broke the coach's back. Looking back, he could see what happened every time his team went to the Final Four or won the national championship. "It's like another tropical storm," he said of the oppressively giddy reaction to his teams' Final Four string. "Oh, boy, here comes another one."

Looking back – everyone looks back, wondering how it is they couldn't see what was happening to Krzyzewski until it was too late – Bilas remembers thinking Krzyzewski kept an incredible schedule, juggling coaching with recruiting back when Bilas himself was being recruited. "During fall practice, he would fly out after (Duke's) practice to watch me play in a pickup game, and then he would catch the red-eye back to Durham," Bilas said. "That caught my attention."

Alarie remembers his coach always having an ailment of one kind or another. Krzyzewski wasn't the kind to complain about it to the players, but they knew. How could they not? "Coach was always dealing with some type of injury," Alarie said. "After practice he was always on the tennis court, and then you'd see him nursing a sore knee, or a sore shoulder, or with a stiff back. But I didn't realize the extent of his back problems until it was an issue."

The back was sore, but the public was demanding, and Krzyzewski listened to the public instead of his protesting body. He was wanted at a coaching clinic? He'd be there. The National Association of Basketball Coaches wanted his input? Let's talk now. Sign an autograph? Hand over the pen. Krzyzewski also made speeches like a politician, the motivational kind to business leaders and the basketball kind to booster clubs. Along the way, a terrible thing happened to Krzyzewski. He lost the killer focus he had used to build Duke from the lean days of the post-Bill Foster era into the deepest program in the country. His recruiting began to slide as the amount of time he had to give prospective players was eaten into by all the speeches and clinics and interviews. Little touches Krzyzewski used to give a recruit, like driving him personally to Raleigh-Durham Airport after a visit to campus just so they could spend a few extra minutes getting to know each other better, were eliminated. Soon he was signing players based as much on what he had seen on tape as what he had seen and felt in person. That is a rocky foundation for a series of relationships that each will last four years and, together, will determine whether a program stays where it is, rises higher, or sinks.

Duke began to sink. And Krzyzewski went down with the ship.

First his tennis game began to suffer. Then, it was racquetball. Pretty soon in the summer of 1994, Krzyzewski could barely walk without pain in his back. Eventually the pain moved into his left leg as well. A doctor told him why: a degenerative disc in his back that required surgery.

The summer had begun badly enough. Krzyzewski had scheduled his team to go on a tour of Australia, but when a number of players reported lackluster grades that spring, Krzyzewski canceled the trip. Krzyzewski had made a strong stand for grades before. He refused to hang up the 1990 Final Four banner because a few seniors from that team didn't graduate, and by 1999, when one 1990 Duke senior still hadn't graduated, that banner still was missing from the rafters of Cameron Indoor Stadium. The cancellation of the Australian trip for academic reasons left Krzyzewski more than embarrassed. He was angry, and he actually was thinking of leaving Duke. The Portland Trail Blazers had offered him millions of dollars to become their coach, and for about a week, Krzyzewski seriously considered it. Finally he announced he was staying at Duke, but he conceded that the canceled Australian trip was a factor in his flirtation with the NBA. "When I had to cancel the trip because (the players) needed to be in summer school, it put me in the mood to look deeper into things," he said.

Now this. Surgery. Krzyzewski put it off as long as he could, but finally the pain was too much and he had the procedure done October 21, about a week after practice had begun. Although he had little choice in the matter because of the pain, it was the wrong time to have the surgery. The presence of Grant Hill on the previous season's Final Four squad had cloaked some shortcomings on the team, and with Hill gone, the bill had come due. The backcourt was weak, without a true point guard to assume the duties Krzyzewski had seen handled exquisitely by Tommy Amaker, Quin Snyder, Bobby Hurley and, somewhat, Hill the previous season. The post players, Eric Meek and Greg Newton, weren't up to the standards set by Christian Laettner, Alaa Abdelnaby, Danny Ferry and Jay Bilas. This was a Duke team in trouble.

So Krzyzewski came back from surgery – too soon. It's as simple as that. Doctors told him to rest for six weeks after the surgery. He rested two days. While at home, recovering from the procedure, Krzyzewski had his staff come over every day after working with the team. They brought him tapes of practice every day, and together the coaches analyzed the team's direction. Krzyzewski was back at the gym a week later, resorting to almost desperate measures just to stay around the team. He watched practice from a special chair or leaned on a lectern when he stood. When Krzyzewski conducted interviews, he often did so lying flat on his back. Sometimes during practice Krzyzewski would get up from his custom-made chair, creep over to the bleachers and lie down. The pain was too much.

Amid all the pain, there was controversy. Joey Beard, the 6'10" sophomore from the Boston area who was hailed as another Christian Laettner or another Danny Ferry, decided he wanted to go to another school. He rarely played as a freshman, his prospects as a sophomore weren't much better, and even worse, he and Krzyzewski were clashing on a daily basis at practice and even in the locker room. Finally, a few days before the first game of the season, Beard told Krzyzewski he was thinking of leaving. Give it some time, Krzyzewski said. Think about it. So Beard thought about it.

A week later, the Blue Devils traveled to Auburn Hills, Michigan, to play No. 16 Connecticut. After the game, a 90-86 Duke loss, Krzyzewski saw Beard on the team bus and asked him if he had thought more about transferring.

Beard said, "I think I'm going to leave."

And Krzyzewski answered, "OK, you're off the team."

The next day when Beard went to the locker room to clean out his locker, he saw that it had been done for him. His nameplate was off the locker. His stuff was in a box next to it. Other than the box, it was as if Joey Beard had never existed, Krzyzewski had other problems.

Five weeks after returning to practice, Krzyzewski boarded a flight and spent nearly ten hours en route to Hawaii. There, in the Rainbow Classic in Honolulu, the Blue Devils lost their first-round game by ten points to unranked Iowa. Suitably discouraged, Krzyzewski ordered an all-night film session for his staff to prepare for the next two games. Duke would win both, against Boston University and Georgia Tech, but at what cost? There are so many questions. What if Duke hadn't gone to Hawaii, trapping Krzyzewski and his sore back in a cross-country, and then some, flight from Durham to Honolulu? What if Duke hadn't lost that first game to Iowa, triggering something very much like panic in the coaching staff? What if the very next night after the team returned home hadn't been New Year's Eve, another night of little sleep for Krzyzewski?

Assistant coach Pete Gaudet doesn't know the answers

to any of those questions. But he knows the Hawaii trip sealed Krzyzewski's fate. "On the flight back from Hawaii ... I just think if you've ever been on one of those flights and felt normal, it's still bad. And he wasn't feeling normal," Gaudet said. "I know he didn't have much sleep over there, with three games in three days, and that was probably really tough. That exacerbated the situation. I mean, he was trying to win some games over there. Then he got no sleep on New Year's Eve. It just got worse and worse."

The ACC season was starting in four days, and Krzyzewski was no longer sleeping well at night. He was barely eating. The pain, the pain. On January 4, 1995, Krzyzewski coached his last game for nearly eleven months. It was a loss, 75-70, as Clemson came into Cameron Indoor Stadium and buried the Blue Devils beneath a fusillade of three-pointers. Two days later, after an off day, the plan was for Duke to practice that afternoon at Cameron and then fly to Atlanta for a game the next night at Georgia Tech. Krzyzewski woke up that morning, showered, and returned to bed. He got up again, shaved, then returned to bed. He got up again, got dressed for practice, then returned to bed again.

Mickie Krzyzewski discovered her husband still in the bedroom, about to be late for practice, struggling to get out the door. According to *Sports Illustrated*, Mickie and Mike had the following conversation:

Mickie: "You're going to the doctor."

Mike: "I'm going to practice. I have appointments with the players."

Mickie: "You don't have the strength." At this, she left the room, called a doctor, then returned. "The appointment's at 2:30, Mike."

Mike: "I have practice at 2:30!"

Mickie: "I'm telling you now: It's me or basketball. If you're not at the doctor's at 2:30, I'll know what you chose."

Mike was at the doctor's at 2:30. But there was no need for the appointment. His doctor took one look at Krzyzewski and had him admitted to Duke Medical Center. There the coach stayed for four days, where a battery of tests showed Krzyzewski was suffering from severe fatigue. The team went to Georgia Tech without him, coached by Gaudet, and lost. Duke lost its next four games as well, all without Krzyzewski, who was miserable at home, trying to get better fast rather than simply trying to get better. At one point, feeling the guilt over not being there with his sinking team, Krzyzewski dragged himself into Athletic Director Tom Butters' office and, like the former West Point captain he had been, offered to go down with the ship: resign. Butters chased him out of the office, assuring him the job was his whenever he was ready to return. On January 22, Duke announced Krzyzewski wouldn't be coming back that season. Before the official announcement, Krzyzewski met with his staff.

"He said, 'I can't do it any more this season,'" Gaudet said. "He said, 'This just isn't getting any better.'"

Krzyzewski tabbed Gaudet as his interim successor. They had been together since 1975, with a three-year interruption beginning when Gaudet replaced Krzyzewski at Army in 1980, but now their friendship and coaching relationship would be tested like never before. It wouldn't pass the test.

Instead of serving as a rallying point, the loss of their head coach seemed to send the Blue Devils off onto their own courses. "We didn't play as a team any more after Coach K went out," said Jeff Capel, a junior guard on that team. "It was like we were all out for ourselves. It wasn't anybody's fault but our own."

Duke would win just four more times that season. After Krzyzewski left with a 9-3 record, the team went 4-15 the rest of the way to finish 13-18, the worst season at Duke since Krzyzewski's third year in Durham in 1982-83. As the team slipped toward the ACC cellar, finding itself in, but losing, close game after close game, Krzyzewski tried to stay out of it. "He told us to go with our instincts," Gaudet said. "We didn't call him, and, for the most part, he didn't call us. He just told us to work things out."

Krzyzewski did stay somewhat in the loop. When 6-foot-7 high school forward Vince Carter of Daytona Beach, Florida, came to Durham for his official visit, Krzyzewski met with him for two hours at his home. Carter, one of the top five high school players in the country, eventually chose North Carolina. Duke suffered another loss to the Tar Heels late that season, one of the more incredible games in the Duke-North Carolina series. Duke rallied from an eight-point deficit in the final seventeen seconds of overtime and forced a second overtime on Capel's 35-footer at the buzzer. North Carolina finally pulled out a 102-100 victory.

Four games into Gaudet's regime, all Duke losses, Duke Sports Information Director Mike Cragg called the NCAA for guidance on a statistical matter: Which coach now gets credit with Duke's wins and losses, Krzyzewski or Gaudet? The NCAA told Cragg it was his call to make, and this is the call he made – Gaudet received credit for the games he coached in Krzyzewski's absence. Krzyzewski wasn't told about the statistical issue until the season was over, Cragg said. "He had more important things on his mind – like life," Cragg said. "It was my decision, not his. I'm not surprised some people ripped us for doing it that way, but it was a double-edged sword. If Duke had gone on to win the national championship, people would have said, 'You can't give that to Krzyzewski, he wasn't even there.'" It was Cragg's decision, but ultimately it was Krzyzewski's call, and he supported Cragg. Gaudet would have the 4-15 finish tagged to his name. Weren't those players the ones Krzyzewski had recruited and signed? Hadn't Krzyzewski coached some of them for as many as three-plus years? Hadn't Krzyzewski been there for the bulk of the practices from October 15 to January 6, when his fatigue finally got the best of him? Few people would suggest Duke was going to finish 13-18 that season with Krzyzewski on the bench and not at home.

If it rankles Gaudet, Gaudet won't say it. He ducks the issue with a joke – "I guess that 4-15 record is going to cost me my spot in the Hall of Fame," he said, "but I'll get over it." – and then politely declines to discuss the issue further.

After the season Krzyzewski dismissed Gaudet from the staff, rather than make the fifty-something Gaudet a recruiting assistant, which is what Gaudet would have had to become had he stayed. Krzyzewski briefly addressed the issue in John Feinstein's *A March to Madness*, in which he is quoted as saying: "I always believed the theory that every staff needs an older coach. One morning I looked in the mirror and realized I was the older coach, whether I wanted to admit it or not."

Krzyzewski knew he was faced with choosing what was best for a friendship, or choosing what was best for his program. He made his choice. Four years later, Gaudet was out of coaching, a teacher in Nashville, Tennessee, hoping to return to the business. By then there appeared to have been some healing on both sides. When Krzyzewski's top assistant in 1999, his former point guard, Quin Snyder, was considering moving on to become a head coach, Snyder had conversations with Gaudet about working together. Had Snyder gone to Vanderbilt, where Gaudet had worked as an assistant, Gaudet almost surely would have joined him. Snyder ultimately took the job at Missouri and went in another direction with his staff. Still, the Snyder-Gaudet conversations suggest the Krzyzewski-Gaudet rift had been closed somewhat. It was as close to a happy ending as the story would get.

Krzyzewski returned for the 1995-96 season, and

bunker mentality had set in. To protect himself from himself as much as anything, Krzyzewski brought in time-management consultants to help him manage his time better. Among the changes: a phone line for strictly family use was installed in the Krzyzewski home, and a new parking space next to Cameron Indoor Stadium was created to let Krzyzewski come and go without having to encounter well-wishers. Motivational speeches and clinics were cut back. Interviews, other than postgame press conferences and weekly teleconferences set by the conference for all the ACC's coaches, were all but eliminated. Mickie Krzyzewski, in charge of her husband's schedule, was nicknamed "The Dragon Lady." She liked it. It meant she was doing her job, protecting her husband. The heck with anyone else. No offense intended.

It wasn't easy, but Krzyzewski had rearranged his priorities. He wouldn't let what happened to him after the 1991 and 1992 national championships happen again. "It was a long and arduous learning process," Mickie said. "The priorities were always there. They've always been the same in terms of family and his relationship with God and his relationship with his players and staff. But so many things got in the way of him carrying out the priorities the way he wanted."

More unhappiness was around the corner. The following fall, during practice for the 1995-96 season, Krzyzewski's mother, Emily, was diagnosed with terminal cancer. Krzyzewski took time off from practice to fly to Chicago to be with his mother, the woman he still called after every game, just to talk, just to hear her voice, the calm after an ACC storm. Cancer? Terminal? Can't be. "He didn't believe it," Mickie Krzyzewski said.

It was not an easy season, not an easy return to his roost. Away from the court, his mother was dying and an aunt, Mary, passed away during the season. She lived in the same house where Mike spent his childhood in Chicago, and in February he flew home the day after a two-point victory against Maryland for her funeral.

That came two weeks after the Krzyzewski family, including the coach, had spent time in Durham Superior Court for the trial of a Durham man charged with robbing Mike's middle daughter, Lindy. The man, who was convicted and sentenced to eight years in prison, had mugged Lindy outside a mall in Durham, taking her purse and her car, a 1993 Honda Civic that was recovered later that night. The verdict wasn't the end of the ordeal, however. After the verdict was announced, the convicted man's sister lunged at Mickie in the courtroom, shouting, "I'm going to get you!" The Durham Police Department posted guards outside the Krzyzewski home for the next several days, and an officer in street clothes sat behind the Duke bench for three games, following the coach to and from the locker room. At Wake Forest, where Lindy was a freshman, campus police provided similar protection. "We'd never been involved in anything like that," Mickie said. "Frankly, it was very frightening."

On the court, the Blue Devils lost one player, starting forward Tony Moore, to grades when he flunked out of school. Another starter, sophomore guard Trajan Langdon, missed the season with a knee injury. A third starter, Carmen Wallace, went down with a season-ending injury in February. The Blue Devils went 18-13 and lost in the first round of the NCAA tournament, a very atypical Duke season and yet an encouraging result considering all that had happened in the previous twelve months.

Mike Krzyzewski was philosophical about it all. "People have these things (happen to them)," he said. "There's just been more things that have happened this year with our team and outside than usually would happen."

The worst thing of all happened the following October, in 1996, when Emily Krzyzewski died at home in Chicago. Mike spent the last week of her life at her side, urging her to exorcise the cancer, to beat it. She couldn't, and

Krzyzewski lost one of his best friends, maybe his very best friend. For years after her death there would be times when, after a particularly emotional game, he would pick up the phone to call his mother, only to quickly hang it up, frustrated and in tears.

After she died, Mike Krzyzewski learned about a secret his mother had been carrying all these years. In a desk in her home, family members found a twenty-year-old notepad Emily Krzyzewski had been keeping since her son became the head coach at Army. She had marked down every game her son's teams had played at Army and later at Duke, noted the opponent and the date and the score, and finished each line with a W or an L. The ledger had 449 Ws and 199 Ls.

Today Krzyzewski has that notepad.

———————

Chapter Eight

NOTHING LASTS
FOREVER

Their names, their names.
College basketball, its
history and its flavor and
its very feel, drips from their names. Bobby Knight. Jim
Valvano. Mike Krzyzewski. Ah, who needs those first names?
Knight. Valvano. Krzyzewski. Recent college basketball in a
nutshell.

Over the years they have created paths and crossed
paths, and their careers have become intertwined in ways
none could have imagined. There has been death and the
destruction of a friendship, and death and the creation of
another. Knight, Valvano, Krzyzewski.

Jim Valvano can talk now only from the grave, but if
you listen closely enough, you can hear one of the final
lessons he learned coming from a voice that sounds very
much like Mike Krzyzewski's. "I never want a time to come
when my family can say, 'You love basketball more than
me,'" Krzyzewski says now.

That is a lesson Krzyzewski learned from Valvano. It is
odd that Krzyzewski could, or would, learn much of
anything from Valvano given their relationship, which

started haltingly in the late 1960s when they were playing in college, competing against each other, and resumed in the mid-1970s when they were coaching in college, competing against each other, and only intensified in 1980 when they made the move within two weeks of one another to the Atlantic Coast Conference, Krzyzewski to Duke, Valvano to N.C. State. When Krzyzewski was Knight's point guard at Army, Valvano was a guard at Rutgers. Their teams played every year, and Valvano and Krzyzewski often guarded each other. When Krzyzewski became the coach at Army, Valvano was coaching at Iona, and in the five games their teams played over the next five years, Valvano had the upper hand, three victories to two.

"It's funny how their career paths kind of attracted each other," Valvano's older brother, Nick, said in 1999. "They wound up showing up in the ACC at about the same time and of course, there the competition only got worse. I wouldn't call them friends at that time, but they were cordial. Cordial competitors, you could say, who would pull their own eyes out to beat you."

Krzyzewski became known as the master coach while Valvano was known for his flamboyance, but it was Valvano who made life for Krzyzewski especially difficult in the early 1980s. While Krzyzewski was struggling at Duke, posting losing seasons in his second and third year there, Valvano averaged twenty-one victories per season in that same stretch and capped it by winning the national title in 1983, the year Duke fans began shouting for Krzyzewski's dismissal. It wasn't enough that Duke had to lose to North Carolina. Now they were being overshadowed by N.C. State as well? It was too much.

Krzyzewski would get his national championship in 1991, and then his second in 1992, but it is interesting to note that both came after Valvano – whose N.C. State teams were 5-5 at Cameron Indoor Stadium, compared to the meager 20-percent success ratio of most visitors – had been forced to resign after the 1990 season by the N.C.

State brass. A book released the previous year had made
N.C. State basketball under Valvano look like a renegade
program full of NCAA violations and worse.

That book was the start of the Krzyzewski-Valvano
friendship. Krzyzewski saw the storm the book had
created and called Valvano in his office.

"Mike was one of the first guys to pick up the phone,"
Nick Valvano said, "and say, 'I know you haven't done
anything wrong. Maybe some things have happened that
have embarrassed you, but I know you, and I'm sticking
by you.'

"Where does a relationship start? Sometimes you don't
know when it starts, but you know when it mushrooms
because it's so obvious. That's when it mushroomed.

"That was the first time Jim had ever seen that side of
Mike. Mike doesn't let a lot of people get close to him, and
Jim certainly wasn't, up to that point. You have to
remember people were ready to tar and feather Jim. It
was an incredible time for Jim. That's when Jim really
started believing Mike was a friend."

If they had met in another life – say, Krzyzewski was
selling shoes at the mall, and Valvano was making pastries
next door – they probably would have been friends from
the start. True, on the outside, they were nothing alike.
Krzyzewski had Polish roots and was conservative, and
Valvano came from Italian ancestry and was a showman at
heart, but inside they were the same. Products of
European immigrant, working-class families. Family men
with three daughters. Loyal. Competitive. Very emotional.
Very proud. Capable of crying in front of their families or
their players.

"Inside, they were like brothers," Nick said. "Mike's
grinding inside with his emotions, you can see it on his
face, coming out of his eyes. Jimmy was throwing his
jacket off and ripping the seat off his pants. The fire's all
the same, you know?"

And then one day doctors told Valvano his fire was
going out. In 1992 he went to the hospital with back pains,

and came out with a diagnosis: cancer. Terminal. Jim Valvano was dying.

Valvano was treated at Duke Hospital. Outside of family members, the person who visited him the most was Krzyzewski. His visits had a galvanizing effect on Valvano. They lasted for hours, rambling conversations that left Valvano's family shaking their heads at the wonder of it all. The Duke coach and the former N.C. State coach – bonding?

"When Jim went into the hospital, Mike would go and visit him every ... single ... day," Nick Valvano said, punctuating the last three words with the same kind of passion that was so evident inside his younger brother. "Not only was it an incredibly nice gesture, but the impact it had on my brother was astounding. His pain would go away, his face would lighten up. They'd talk about practice, they'd talk about recruiting, they'd talk about things that, outside of their families, were the most important things in their lives. Everyone else wanted to talk about the chemo and the cancer. Mike let Jim forget about that stuff."

And Jim let Mike see the road he was traveling, at Duke, was treacherous and cruel. Mickie Krzyzewski knows better than anyone the impact Valvano had on her husband. "What Jimmy told Mike was, 'I didn't do it right. I was really wrong. Don't screw it up,'" Mickie said.

Krzyzewski was listening. Said his oldest daughter, Debbie, "He was able to say, 'No, I have to go to my daughter's basketball game tonight,' or, 'No, I'm having dinner at home tonight.' Jimmy taught him that."

A few months before he died, Valvano attended a Duke practice and spoke to the Blue Devils after it was over. His message was spoken out loud, but it didn't have to be. His message was delivered the moment he walked into the gym, so slim, his thick mane of jet-black hair gone, his booming voice reduced to a scratchy whisper. His message was this: Life can change. Do everything you possibly can do ... and do it today.

Valvano died April 28, 1993. He was forty-seven.

Krzyzewski was forty-six. According to Nick Valvano, Krzyzewski reached the hospital room shortly after Jim had died. He was the only person not in Valvano's family to be there. He is a part of the family now.

"I love Mike so much, he's like a brother to me," Nick said. "It's a very special thing. I've always felt that people never really knew who Jim was. He was taken from us too soon, before they could see there was a heck of a lot more there than the showman. What I see right now, I'm so happy, because people are getting an opportunity to see the real Coach K. He's here, and he's almost the same age Jim would be. I'm telling you, they're so much alike as people, not necessarily looks or personalities, but their core values are so much alike. For people to think Mike Krzyzewski is only this tough coach ... They don't have the opportunity to see the compassionate, serious, loving guy – and he'll kill me for calling him a loving man – but everyone should know the man Jim was. That's the man Mike is."

Near the end, Jim Valvano asked Krzyzewski to go to Washington, D.C. to speak to nine North Carolina representatives in Congress about the need for more funding for cancer research. "You've got to make it happen," Valvano told Krzyzewski. "Go make it happen."

Valvano died the day before the conference, but his family members asked that Krzyzewski keep the engagement, which he did. "Our efforts are going well, but it pales in comparison with what is needed," Krzyzewski told the lawmakers. "Federal funding is needed."

Today Krzyzewski is a board member for the private V Foundation, which began shortly after Valvano died and, in its first six years, had raised more than $8 million to fund forty-eight doctors and the construction of three cancer research facilities around the country.

"We're getting there," said Nick Valvano, who, in 1999, moved to Raleigh to become the chief executive officer of the V Foundation. "This is something a lot of people believe in. I know Mike believes in it so strongly."

178 / Nothing Lasts Forever

Valvano's impact on Krzyzewski was there six years after his death. On the night stand next to his bed at home in Durham, Krzyzewski has a copy of the *Sports Illustrated* magazine with Valvano on the cover and a story on the dying coach inside. The story is totally marked up. Krzyzewski went after it with a highlighter, underlining parts that reminded him of Valvano's lessons. Six years later, Krzyzewski still looks at the magazine.

Sometimes, you wonder, does Krzyzewski ever think of Valvano – and mourn the loss of another good friend? Does he mourn the loss of Bobby Knight?

Almost thirty years before it finally unraveled, Krzyzewski's relationship with Knight began in the living room of Bill and Emily Krzyzewski's two-flat in their Polish-American neighborhood of Chicago. That was where Knight, acting on a tip from a Chicago high school coach who had recommended he take a look at Krzyzewski, first met the boy who would become a man playing for him at Army. Knight was basically the only Division I basketball coach offering Krzyzewski any sort of scholarship. He was showing Krzyzewski the dream, and offering a chance to make it come true. Grudgingly, Krzyzewski took it.

From that point on, theirs was a complex relationship, as are so many of the relationships Knight has. This is a man whose idea of instruction is to curse in his player's face, then throw him out of practice. Knight's idea of humor is joking with the national media about taking a bullwhip to one of his players. Knight's idea of a protest is to fling a chair across the basketball court. And his idea of diplomacy is to not so subtly accuse a referee, as he did in 1998 with referee Ted Valentine, of taking a personal agenda onto the court every time that referee officiated an Indiana game. Valentine, as it happens, is somewhat in the middle of the mess that spelled the beginning of the end of the friendship between Krzyzewski and Knight. A complex man, Knight.

They once were terribly close. Knight treated Krzyzewski as he did most of his players, haranguing the future Duke coach when he was a mere Army point guard, telling him he couldn't shoot worth a darn, punctuating that thought by threatening to break Krzyzewski's arm if he shot too much. But Knight treated him with respect, too. Krzyzewski digested every bit of Knight's debasement, and Knight respected him enough to make him captain of his team. It was Knight who handed Krzyzewski the phone in the Army locker room on the night in 1969 that Krzyzewski's father died of a heart attack, it was Knight who hurriedly packed his things so he could accompany Krzyzewski to Chicago for the funeral, and it was Knight who hung around the Krzyzewski home in Chicago, offering any and all services to Emily as she prepared to bury her husband.

Later, it was Knight who gave Krzyzewski his first collegiate coaching job, putting him on the staff at his burgeoning Indiana powerhouse, and it was Knight, who one year later, recommended to the Army athletic hierarchy that it make the 27-year-old, unproven Krzyzewski its head coach. Knight also made a strong pitch to Duke to hire Krzyzewski five years later after Krzyzewski had turned down a job offer from Iowa State – which also had come calling after a recommendation from Knight.

At Duke, Krzyzewski credits Knight with giving him a solid piece of counsel right off the bat. "I was already recruiting nationally at Army," Krzyzewski said, "but the people at Duke said, 'It's different here. It's more restricted.' I said, 'Are you kidding me? Here I won't have to sell a kid on spending five years in the army and driving a tank.' Coach Knight told me all the players we'd be looking at (at Duke) will look better than the ones we had at Army – but we're not playing Army's schedule, either. He was making the point that you have to look at the level of play in your league and make sure you recruit kids who can win there, not just be satisfied with players that were better than anyone I could have signed at Army. That was a great piece of advice."

Even so, Krzyzewski did his best to distance himself from his former boss when he took over at Duke. Reporters searched for the Bobby Knight in this Bobby Knight disciple, but Krzyzewski wouldn't play along. "Bobby Knight had a tremendous influence on me, but I'm not Bobby Knight," Krzyzewski said at his introductory Duke press conference in 1980. "You make a mistake when you try to be someone other than yourself. I'm a different person than Knight, and I'll run my own program."

He did, but still, the Knight connection was there. Consider that March weekend in 1986 when Duke reached its first Final Four under Krzyzewski and Knight was there, in Dallas, speaking to the Blue Devils before their national semifinal against Kansas and strutting around the coliseum later like a peacock, showing off his allegiance to Duke by wearing a Blue Devils pin on his sweater. Duke was stunned by Louisville in the national title game, and Knight repeatedly called Krzyzewski the following week, offering consolation. The next year, on its way to the national title, Indiana beat Duke in the Sweet Sixteen round of the NCAA tournament, and afterward Knight opened his postgame press conference with: "It's hard for me to enjoy this very much thinking about Mike."

By 1992, something had changed. It could have been something as obvious as this: Duke, not Indiana, had reached its fifth straight Final Four, and Krzyzewski, not Knight, was considered the preeminent coach of the pre-eminent program in the country. It could have been something less transparent, something as hard to prove as Knight's theory, spoken to buddies, that Krzyzewski had forgotten about his friend and mentor as the tag "coaching genius" had been placed upon him. Whatever it was, their relationship crashed onto jagged rocks that year in the Final Four, when Duke beat Indiana 81-78.

Immediately after the final horn, Krzyzewski approached Knight for what he thought would be a hug.

He thought wrong. Knight brushed past Krzyzewski, offering only a quick, formal handshake, but stopped to embrace one of Krzyzewski's staff members, Col. Tom Rogers, a former assistant for Knight at Army. Krzyzewski was stung, and that sting worsened several minutes later when he and Knight passed each other behind the press conference podium and Knight again brushed past Krzyzewski but stopped to shake hands with another member of the Duke entourage, this time Christian Laettner. Krzyzewski, according to John Feinstein's book *A March to Madness*, was emotionally blindsided. He saw his wife Mickie later in the locker room and began crying. When she asked what was wrong, Krzyzewski could only blurt out one word:

"Knight."

Those are some of the facts, about the only ones out there for public consumption. Beyond that, Krzyzewski won't talk about what happened to his relationship with Knight, and Knight won't talk about it, either. Friends of Knight, former Indiana player Steve Alford and former Indiana top assistant Dan Dakich, both said in 1999 that they consider Krzyzewski to be their friend. About the only thing Knight has said publicly about Krzyzewski, since 1992, is this comment he made to an Indiana sports writer in 1998: "The best coach in the country is Mike Krzyzewski. He runs the best program, gets the best players, and does the best possible job with those players." Krzyzewski is similarly respectful, referring to his former boss as "Coach Knight."

For perspective on this tricky Krzyzewski-Knight issue, understand what happened that day in 1992 at the Final Four. Indiana led 39-27 in the first half, but Duke rallied behind, among other things, an enormous edge at the foul line. Duke shot forty-two free throws and made twenty-eight, compared to sixteen attempts and twelve conversions for the Hoosiers. Five players fouled out – four from Indiana, its top four scorers in the game. At one point in the second half, Indiana had been called for nine fouls,

Duke one, and Knight was screaming at referee Ted Valentine. Late in the game Valentine apparently had heard enough, and he called a technical on Knight that helped seal the Hoosiers' fate.

About a year later the media began to get wind of the brewing storm clouds over the once-amicable relationship of two of the better coaches in college basketball. Krzyzewski tried to deflate the issue, but privately he told associates, "Bobby's friends need to tell him when he's wrong." A few years later when Indiana and Duke met in the 1996 Preseason NIT in New York City, Krzyzewski felt Knight blatantly tried to toy with his head during pregame warmups. Krzyzewski stood in front of the Indiana bench, waiting for Knight to emerge from the locker room, waiting for the pregame handshake. He waited, and waited, and waited. The starting lineups were introduced, and still Knight hadn't appeared. Not long before the opening tap, Knight came out of the locker room with an old friend, draped his arm around that friend, and offered Krzyzewski a quick squeeze of the fingers before moving on. Indiana won that game 85-69, and Knight was gracious at the conclusion, giving Krzyzewski a more sincere handshake.

Afterward, Krzyzewski was unburdened by what he felt was a pregame blowoff. "I'm almost glad it happened that way," Krzyzewski said in *A March to Madness*. "It lets me put a period on the end of the sentence: The end."

Besides, life was too short to worry about such things. By that night in 1996, Jim Valvano had already taught Krzyzewski that.

———————

Chapter Nine

CRAZY FOR KRZYZEWSKI

At Cameron Indoor Stadium, quiet hurts. Inside the gym, where Duke officials shoehorn 9,314 people in for games, the noise ricochets off the floor and off the low ceiling and against the rather tight walls and gets louder and louder until your ears, on the right night, feel like they are on fire. The place is loud up to an hour before tipoff, especially if the North Carolina Tar Heels are the opponent, and it stays loud through the entire game. There are no lulls, other than the respectful silence that comes when Duke players shoot foul shots. It is so loud here that leaving the gym and going into the nearby interview area can be painful to the ear drums, the sudden absence of volume a shock – something like a deep-sea diver whose body gets accustomed to the pressure of the sea, but who must slowly float to the surface lest the sudden absence of pressure do nasty tricks to the body.

It is named after Eddie Cameron, the former Duke basketball and football coach who also served for years as athletic director. It is a palace of browns and grays, the brick pattern mimicking the look of almost every other building on campus. From the outside, Cameron Indoor Stadium could in fact be mistaken for just another building on campus. A library, maybe. A chapel. It is so short, so humble-looking, so misleading to the eye, that from the outside the arena doesn't look like an arena at all. More than a few first-time visitors have stood outside its doors, asking passersby for directions to the building that would crush them if it collapsed at that very moment.

The shrine is inside. Crystal trophies from the national championships of 1991 and 1992, rich, wood plaques honoring the All-Americans who have played here, more brass than you have ever seen in your life. Down a slender hallway is Mike Krzyzewski's office, but to get there you must first be introduced to the teams that produced the foundation for this program. Photos of every Duke team that has won an Atlantic Coast Conference title, going back to the 1950s, line the walls, including the later groups that won with Krzyzewski. Grant Hill and Antonio Lang, who played on ACC champions in 1991, 1992 and 1994, grow older, year by year, right before your eyes. "I love that place," Lang said of Cameron. "It's just something special, and to play there is like a dream. Anyone who grows up playing basketball has to dream of playing at Cameron Indoor Stadium. If you don't, you just don't know college basketball."

Said Krzyzewski: "Since I've started coaching here, I've always known I coached not just at a great school, but a special arena. Cameron is one of the best in all of sports. It's a building, but it's got a soul."

There are rumors here, rumors of shenanigans being perpetrated by Krzyzewski, rumors of edges sought in creative ways. North Carolina players and coaches, for example, swear that Krzyzewski turns up the heat inside the arena on the nights of games, especially when his team has more depth than that year's version of the Tar

Heels. They also say that Krzyzewski turns down the heat in the visitors' locker room, making the impact on the warm court that much more debilitating. "I have to wear my sweats in the locker room, and I don't take them off until right before we come out to shoot," North Carolina senior forward Ademola Okulaja said before the 1999 game at Cameron. "It's not cold in there. It's freezing. And then you go out on the court and it's like an oven."

All tomfoolery – real and imagined – aside, the place has its charm. It is charming, for example, that Duke Athletic Director Joe Alleva, Tom Butters' replacement in 1998, has a wall air-conditioning unit hanging from his window because the in-house air doesn't always work. It is charming, too, that a nest of birds always seems to find its way to the rafters, and that the birds come out and play during the mornings and afternoons, when the gym is mostly quiet. The birds do not come out during games. Too loud.

Blame it on the Crazies. The Cameron Crazies are just as much a part of Cameron Indoor Stadium as Krzyzewski and Christian Laettner and the rest. Through the years Krzyzewski has maintained an interesting, often adversarial, but predominantly affectionate relationship with the Crazies. They even named their student shantyville after him, giving the title "Krzyzewski-ville" to the rows and rows of tents that pop up outside the arena before every North Carolina game. Sometimes the tents are set up months in advance to get tickets, the rule being that each tent must be occupied at all times by at least one dweller or otherwise risk losing its place in line. There are no showers here. There are no sinks. No bathrooms.

Krzyzewski loves Krzyzewski-ville.

"What an honor," he said. "It is such an honor to have something named after you that is so alive, so full of life, so vital. It's one of the better honors I've ever had, really."

Krzyzewski-ville is where the Duke students scheme for hours and hours, weeks and weeks, for just the right chants to unleash on the Tar Heels. In 1999 when two North Carolina team members – assistant coach Dave Hanners and starting freshman forward Jason Capel – came down with mononucleosis and Capel had to watch the game in street clothes, the Crazies chanted, "Dave and Jason, sitting in a tree...," over and over.

The night before Duke plays North Carolina at Cameron Indoor Stadium, Krzyzewski ventures into Krzyzewski-ville and leads the students out of there like some sort of Nike-clad pied piper. The students join him inside Cameron, filing into the same seats where they will create havoc for the Tar Heels in twenty-four hours, and listen to Krzyzewski talk. Sometimes he talks for an hour, about his team, about the Crazies, about their role on his team. Once before the North Carolina game Krzyzewski spoke for an hour, then paused, then capped his speech with the following, goosebump-raising promise:

"I'm going to tell you what I told our team earlier today. We're going to win tomorrow night."

———

Krzyzewski and the Crazies don't always see things the same way. During the 1998-99 season, Michigan came to Durham led by point guard Robbie Reid. His father, Roger Reid, for years had been the coach at Brigham Young University before being ousted after the 1996-97 season for, among other things, scolding a Mormon player from California for "letting down nine million Mormons" by not signing with BYU. The player? Chris Burgess. The school he did sign with? Duke.

As Reid shot free throws at one point in the game, the Crazies began chant-taunting, "Burgess got your dad fired, Burgess got your dad fired." Burgess, sitting on the bench at the time, looked up at the Crazies with a hurt, confused look on his face. Krzyzewski hopped off the bench (fairly impressively for a guy with pending hip replacement surgery, at that) and shouted, "No! Stop that! That's not funny!"

A few years earlier, as Duke was routing a Maryland team led by All-American forward Joe Smith, the Crazies succumbed to the oft-used chant, "Over-rated." Krzyzewski waved at them to stop, and then afterward blasted the Crazies to the media for spending too much energy rooting against the other team and not enough rooting for Duke. "This team is fifteen and one, and no one at Duke seems to know it," he said. "We take it for granted that we're going to win. Don't take it for granted, because it may not always be there. Where are the cheers for (Duke players) Chris Collins and Jeff Capel and the others when they're doing good? This is a great team, a neat bunch of kids. They aren't being appreciated."

Still, there is a mutual respect between Krzyzewski and the dwellers of Krzyzewski-ville, who, in 1994, when Krzyzewski was considering leaving Duke for the Portland Trail Blazers, planted "Stay, Coach K" banners all over campus and also wrote almost a thousand letters to the coach urging him to stay. During the 1997-98 season, Wake Forest center Loren Woods was suspended by Demon Deacons coach Dave Odom for several weeks for health reasons that were more mental than physical. Woods was reinstated in time for the Deacons' game at Duke, the timing of which concerned Krzyzewski. Before the game he went into the stands and asked the Crazies to take it easy on Woods. Chants and taunts may have been ready, but they weren't heard. The Crazies obeyed Krzyzewski.

They obeyed because they knew Krzyzewski honestly felt the students at Duke were an integral part of the team's success, giving Duke one of the premier home-court advantages in the country, regardless of the talent level on the floor. Indeed, Duke ended the 1998-99 season with a 36-game home winning streak, the longest in Atlantic Coast Conference history. Duke ended that season with a 594-135 record (81.5 percent) at Cameron, the sixth-most victories of any school at a current home court. Under Krzyzewski that winning percentage had jumped to 84.9 (236-42), which could explain why he walked into the gym, into a packed house, for a pep rally after the 1991 national championship, looked at the students sitting there, and said simply, "So, where should we put the banner?"

———————

You don't have to believe the Crazies help Duke win basketball games, and that's fine. Maybe they don't. It is an unprovable theory either way in any event, but about this there is no denying: Listen long enough, and the Crazies will make you laugh. They'll make you cringe with embarrassment and possibly boil with anger, but they definitely will make you laugh, too. They make visiting coaches chuckle all the time, including Michigan's Brian Ellerbe, whose Wolverines were whipsawed 108-64 in December 1998 at Cameron. Midway through the first half, when Krzyzewski began spilling reserves all over the court, the Crazies broke into a chant of "two teams, no team, two teams, no team" as they pointed back and forth from the Duke side to the Michigan side. Despite having his shorthandedness pointed out by 9,314 strangers, Ellerbe had to put a hand to his mouth to stifle a grin.

Sometimes the Crazies aren't so funny. When Maryland's Herman Veal visited in 1984 shortly after being accused in an incident involving a coed, the Crazies threw panties and condoms at him and unrolled a picture of a nude woman. Everyone from Maryland coach Lefty Driesell to Duke President Terry Sanford was outraged, Sanford enough to publicly decry the students' behavior. Suitably chastised, the Crazies were warm and fuzzy to the next opponent, which happened to be North Carolina. "A HEARTY WELCOME TO COACH DEAN SMITH AND THE NORTH CAROLINA TAR HEELS" read signs all over Cameron Indoor Stadium. "WELCOME HONORED GUESTS" read others. When North Carolina players shot free throws, the Crazies held aloft placards that said, "Please Miss." And when the Crazies did deign to open their mouths, they chanted things like, "We must question the integrity of the officials."

Krzyzewski usually is too wrapped up in the game to notice exactly what the Crazies are doing, but afterward, when he reviews the games on film, he often plays the audio so he can listen to the Duke students.

"Sometimes when we wouldn't know what the students were chanting, we'd listen to the tape, and Mike would literally stop the meeting," remembers former Duke assistant Pete Gaudet. "He'd take a big sigh and say, 'Aren't they great?'And then we'd listen some more, and there would be something even better later.

"I remember my first week at Duke, people were saying, 'You'll love it, the fans are so creative.' My macho feeling was, 'Hey, I'm a coach, we won't pay attention to that. We won't even see that stuff.' Ten minutes into my first game, here I am chuckling about something. I'm saying to myself, 'Wow, get back to coaching.'"

The Crazies are just so ... crazy. They've worn skull caps to mimic the balding Driesell. They've counted to ten, in German, to Washington's Detlef Schrempf and Christian Welp. Against one ACC foe, one Crazy hopped out of the stands, paraded around the court dressed like a woman and butchered a few bars of the national anthem – a barb at the opposing coach, whose wife sometimes sang the anthem at home.

———

As much affection as he has for the students at Duke, one of the uglier incidents in Krzyzewski's tenure with the Blue Devils centered around a group of students working for *The Chronicle*, the school paper. After the paper assigned mid-season grades to every player on the team – starting forward Greg Koubek got a B, for example, and none received worse than a C-plus – Krzyzewski invited the responsible reporters and editors into the locker room for a chat. He chewed them out for eight minutes. "You can interpret (anything) any way you want because you have freedom of the press," Krzyzewski told the journalists in front of the team. "But it is also my freedom of speech to tell you what I think. I think your article ... is full of *?@#!*, OK? I'm not looking for puff pieces or anything like that, but you're whacked out and you don't appreciate what the *?@#!* is going on and it really *?@#!* me off."

Oops. The profanity-laced diatribe was captured on tape by one reporter, then played for the Durham paper, which ran a story on the incident. It became national news, and the general take was this: Krzyzewski was a bully. Distraught, Krzyzewski apologized to Athletic Director Tom Butters for embarrassing the school and also to the paper for cursing. In waving off the incident, Butters also indicated he was less than thrilled with the entire episode. "I've never known him to do anything that didn't have a reason," Butters said of Krzyzewski. "If there's a problem, I'll handle it and nobody will know anything about it."

Krzyzewski later told *Sports Illustrated*, "I wasn't trying to control the press. I just wanted to say, 'Here are the kids you're grading. Here are their faces. When you write, you're writing about people.' My language wasn't good. But I was disturbed that we had gotten to the point where their fellow students were instruments of entertainment and ego indulgence."

Besides, Krzyzewski added, Greg Koubek deserved an A.

Krzyzewski swung and missed that day with the student journalists at *The Chronicle*, a rare whiff for a middle-aged man who has related so well to his players. He is a part-time philosopher – "Put a plant in a jar and it will fill the jar," he tells his players, "but let it grow on its own and it will grow big enough to fill twenty jars"– and a full-time button-pusher, knowing how far he can go with this player, and how far he cannot go with that one.

"He yells. Definitely. He coaches by feel," said ESPN's Jay Bilas, who played and coached at Duke under Krzyzewski. "Like with me, he would yell at me because he knew I could handle it. But he wouldn't yell at Mark Alarie, because Mark was a different type player, and he probably wouldn't have responded to it. He was different with every player, because every player is different."

In the early 1980s Krzyzewski was growing as a motivator, tinkering with ideas. Bilas remembers playing Louisville in 1982 when Duke started four freshmen and a sophomore. The Cardinals, two years removed from the national championship, were ranked No. 9. Duke had a 6-5 record and was going nowhere. "Before the game, we're sitting in the locker room and all the lights go off," Bilas said. "Coach K walks in with a candle in front of his face, and the only thing illuminated is his face. It was kind of spooky. Then he said, 'I came not to praise Louisville, but to bury them.' Everyone jumped out of their chairs and went sprinting onto the floor, and we ended up jumping the Doctors of Dunk for a ten-point lead. They ended up beating us, so it wasn't like we got a win out of it, but that gimmick was good for a ten-point lead early in the game for a bunch of freshmen.

"I hesitate telling that story, because he was not a 'gimmick' coach. He reasoned with you more than anything. He explained that if you did something this way, and then something else this way, then that would happen, and it would be good. And sure enough, if you did it like he said, it would work out like he said it would."

But still ... the gimmicks. They were so good. For years before the North Carolina game at Cameron Indoor Stadium, Krzyzewski would gather his team around in the locker room and hold a single basketball in the air. Marty Clark, who played at Duke from 1991 to 1994, didn't know what was going on the first time he saw Krzyzewski holding that ball in the air. "He said, 'You see this ball? It doesn't say Wilson on it. It says Krzyzewski,'" Clark said. "And then he'd roll it across the floor and dive on it. And then he'd say, 'That's how much you have to want this game.'"

Same thing, every year. Always before the North Carolina game. "He'd dive for it right there on the floor, right in front of all of us," said Antonio Lang, who also played at Duke from 1991 to 1994. "He didn't care. It's funny now to talk about it, but believe me, it wasn't funny at the time. No one was laughing."

Lang was crying after the final game of his career, the 1994 national championship game, a 76-72 loss to Arkansas, a game decided by Scotty Thurman's three-pointer in the final minute. Lang was the Duke player guarding Thurman at the time. "After the game," Lang said, "the first thing I said was, 'It's my fault, my fault.' Then Coach said, 'We win as a team, and we lose as a team. It wasn't your fault, so don't say that.' That always stuck out. The man had just lost the national championship game, and it was my guy who hit the shot that beat us, and he was worried more about how I was taking it than being disappointed in the loss."

He could be tough. He has thrown the entire team out of practice too many times to count, and he also has scheduled a midnight practice after a four-hour bus ride home from Virginia, where, in 1991, the eventual national champion Blue Devils suffered an 81-64 whipping. In 1986, after a victory that left Krzyzewski baffled by his team's lack of effort, Duke's players returned to the locker room to find their individual pictures, which had been fixed above their lockers, had been thrown in the garbage. Krzyzewski has cracked two chalkboards at halftime, once in Minneapolis, in the 1991 NCAA tournament opener against Southeastern Louisiana, and again in the 1992 national championship game against Michigan.

If *The Chronicle* story says anything about Krzyzewski, it is this: He is better at building students up than tearing

them down. In 1991 North Carolina trashed the Blue
Devils 96-74 in the ACC tournament, and when Duke's
players climbed onto the bus, they found Krzyzewski
waiting for them. "We're going to win the national championship," he said. And then, for emphasis, he looked at
every player on the team and said it again. "We're going to
win the national championship."

Three weeks later, they won the national championship.

Between the prediction and the payoff came the Final
Four game against undefeated Nevada-Las Vegas, already
being called one of the greatest teams of all time. As he
was leaving the locker room for his day-before-the-game
press conference, Krzyzewski told his team he was going
to give the media what it wanted to hear, that UNLV was
an incredible team, and that his Blue Devils would have
little chance at beating them. "Don't listen to any of that,"
Krzyzewski told his players. "I'm telling you right now, we
can win this game." Later that day Krzyzewski fired up his
team by showing each player a personal highlight reel
assistant coach Pete Gaudet had put together. Duke won
that game.

The next year, when Duke had gone from the hunter to
the hunted, and a spot in history possibly awaited them as
the Blue Devils rolled into the 1992 Final Four, Krzyzewski
wasn't afraid to let his team know how good it could be.
"He'd compare us to other teams in the past," Clark said.
"He'd talk about the great UCLA teams, things like that,
and ask us, 'How do you want your names collectively to
be remembered? Do you want everyone to remember
these teams as being special? Then let's be special.' I think
from that moment it didn't matter that we were favored to
win those games. We weren't going to be caught by
surprise by anyone. We were ready to make our mark."

Hey, even if that little spiel hadn't worked, Krzyzewski
always could have dived on a ball. Or lit a candle.
Something.

Chapter Ten

BACK, AND BETTER
THAN EVER

You don't just get here from there, not when here is 37-2 and a spot in the national championship game, and when there is 13-18 and a spot in the Atlantic Coast Conference cellar, and you don't just do it in a measly four years, on will power alone. Not even when you're Mike Krzyzewski, builder of dynasties. No, you don't simply get here from there, just ... because.

What you need is a bridge, and Duke had one. Make that two. One stood 6 feet, 3 inches, the other 5 feet, 11 inches. Their names: Trajan Langdon and Steve Wojciechowski. That's how you get from here to there if you're Mike Krzyzewski. And if you're Mike Krzyzewski, you're very aware of that.

"Wojo and Trajan over the last five years were the bridge to get us back to the elite status," Krzyzewski said in 1999. "I'll forever be indebted to them. They did more than just play. They led, they worked, and more than anything they were committed to me and to Duke basketball. Those kids were my leaders. They led every second."

They couldn't have been more different,

Wojciechowski and Langdon. Langdon was the pure shooter whose every move on the court seemed effortless, right down to those wrist-flicked 21-foot jump shots. Wojciechowski was the bulldog, the caricature of the grinding point guard who made everything he did on the court seem taxing. Which, to him, at the ACC level, it was. The most notable trait they shared was that each was a cultural contradiction, a basketball oxymoron. Wojciechowski was the white kid who toughened his game on the inner city courts of Washington, D.C., where his mother would drop him off for pickup games and then come back a few hours later to take him home to their suburb in Severna Park, Maryland. Langdon was the product of a mixed marriage in Anchorage, Alaska, of all places, blazing a trail where none had been before, drawing college basketball coaches to a state where they had come previously only for the preseason tournament called the Great Alaska Shootout. A recruit in Alaska? A minority recruit? Hey, there's a first time for everything.

"I imagine there weren't too many people like Trajan up in Alaska, and I'm not talking about his basketball, if you know what I mean," said always honest Duke forward Chris Carrawell, who played his own role in the renovation of the Blue Devils' basketball program. "But the guy's popular up there. He could be governor up there, you know what I'm saying?"

Wojciechowski's and Langdon's first season was the 13-18 disaster of 1994-95, the year Krzyzewski went out after twelve games due to exhaustion. The season was traumatic for no Duke player more than Wojciechowski, who lost his high school coach and mentor, Ray Mullins, that winter to cancer and learned his father, Ed Wojciechowski Sr., also was suffering from cancer. "In one year I lost my high school coach, then I lost my college coach – in a way, you know what I mean – and also my dad was in danger," Wojciechowski said. "I was a mess."

The Cameron Crazies weren't sympathetic. Actually,

they didn't know about any of Wojciechowski's off-court problems. Nobody did. He didn't tell anyone but Krzyzewski. As Wojciechowski, a high school All-American, struggled to adapt to the faster, stronger college game, the Cameron Crazies booed him. Four years later they had adopted him as one of their favorites, barking in appreciation as he hounded the opposing point guard up and down the floor.

But again, you don't just get from here to there. From boos to barks? That took some work on Wojo's part. Krzyzewski treated all his players differently, and Langdon and Wojciechowski were prime examples. Langdon was the two-sport star who played minor-league baseball in the summers for the San Diego Padres, the mature-beyond-his-years Yoda who didn't say much and didn't have to be told much, either. Langdon was the kind of player who would work out on his own and not tell anyone, not caring if Krzyzewski or anyone else knew how much effort he was putting into extra shooting drills or solitary rides on a stationary bike. Langdon knew he was putting the work in. That's all that mattered. Krzyzewski knew, too, and, for the most part, he left Langdon alone.

Wojciechowski was another story, not so much because he needed to be pushed, but because he needed to be pushed hard. After his sophomore season, a year in which the Blue Devils, with Krzyzewski now back, went 18-13, Wojciechowski and Krzyzewski had a heart-to-heart talk in the coach's office. Even with Langdon out for the season as a redshirt because of a knee injury, Wojciechowski couldn't crack the starting lineup. He was going to be a junior, and Krzyzewski was starting to wonder if the stocky little guy was ever going to be the kind of leader he demanded his point guard to be. Thus, the meeting.

"I told Steve that if he wanted to play for me, he'd have to become a better shooter, he'd have to get quicker, and just as important, he'd have to be more of a leader than ever," Krzyzewski said. "If he could do those things, he could be my point guard."

Wojciechowski could do those things. He came back for his junior season ten pounds lighter and more than ten percentage points better on shots from the floor (44.3 percent compared to 31.8 percent as a sophomore) and three-point range (39.4 percent to 27.9). He was a second-team All-ACC selection. Langdon, because of the redshirt season now one year of eligibility behind his recruiting classmate, was back for his sophomore season and now a first-team All-ACC shooting guard. Duke, with the gritty Carrawell providing heart and emotion and a silky-smooth St. John's transfer named Roshown McLeod providing inside offense to complement Langdon on the outside, went 24-9 and won the ACC regular-season title, Krzyzewski's fifth.

Duke was back. Notice the punctuation there. That's a period you see at the end of the sentence. Krzyzewski, armed with a seven-year, renewable contract he had signed that summer, already had gone looking for an exclamation point. He didn't find one.

He found four.

———————

It was, almost everyone agreed at the time, the greatest recruiting class in the history of college basketball. It was better than Michigan's Fab Five, quality over quantity. It was unquestionably better than Krzyzewski's first mother lode, the 1986 quartet of Dawkins, Alarie, Bilas and Henderson.

It was: Elton Brand, William Avery, Shane Battier and Chris Burgess. The class had everything – a combination point-shooting guard (the 6-foot-2 Avery), a small forward (the 6'8" Battier), a power forward (the 6'8," 265-pound Brand) and a center (the 7-foot Burgess). It had the top recruit in the country, although which recruit that was could be debated. Some said Battier. Others, Brand. Others, Burgess. Avery, meanwhile, was a top-twenty recruit himself, and in hindsight, he was vastly underrated.

"I still can't believe he got all four of those guys," Virginia coach Pete Gillen said nearly eighteen months later, during the 1998-99 season. "Almost anybody would have been happy to get one, and he got all four. It's ridiculous."

It was the only way. The only way for Duke to get back where it had been earlier in the decade, when it won back-to-back national championships with teams so deep, there were future NBA lottery picks coming off the bench. Krzyzewski was aware of his mistakes of the mid-1990s, when his recruiting slipped and so did the rest of the program. It was a slide heightened in drama – but by no means totally created – by his medical problems of 1995.

"When I had a realization of how bad we were and some of the mistakes I'd made to put us in that position, it was very discouraging," Krzyzewski said. "We were going to have to take some hits, I knew that. But we were going to get back to where we were, too. It wasn't a matter of confidence. It was the only alternative. It wasn't going to be any other way. If you want to get something done, you can't have a bunch of alternatives. You have to have absolutes. I just felt it should get back to where it was.

"You don't get to that level without relying on good players. I'm fortunate I'm at a school and a conference that attracts really good talent, and our staff – especially Quin (Snyder), but David (Henderson) and Johnny (Dawkins) – works very hard to bring that talent in."

With that recruiting class, it was back. Overnight, Duke was as deep as any team in the country. Better than that. Duke was as deep as any two teams in the country. Five former high school All-Americans were on the court when the game started, and seven more were on the bench. It was, as Virginia's Gillen said, ridiculous. Duke began the 1997-98 season ranked third in the country, never slipped lower than that, and finished No. 1. The Blue Devils even had the eventual national champions on the ropes, leading Kentucky by seventeen points with less than ten minutes to play in the East regional final before succumbing, seeing their season end one week short of their goal of a national championship.

It was the final game of Wojciechowski's career, an ending that left him in tears, but at least it didn't almost kill him. That's what seemed to have happened three weeks earlier at the ACC tournament in Greensboro, North Carolina, where Wojciechowski played despite suffering from illness – shades of Bobby Hurley in the 1991 NCAA title game – and afterward, in the shower, collapsed from dehydration and had to be pumped back to action by IVs at a local hospital, where he stayed overnight.

"The program is in good hands," Wojciechowski said. "We wanted to win the national championship this year, but there's next year, and even though I won't be there to enjoy it, the team will be loaded."

The Blue Devils were a force, and so was Krzyzewski. He flexed some of his on-campus clout late that season when Duke President Nan Keohane began zeroing in on a replacement for Athletic Director Tom Butters, who previously had announced the 1997-98 school year would be his last. Keohane wanted to go outside the university. Krzyzewski wanted the job to stay within the family, with assistant AD Joe Alleva, who essentially had been running the department the past few years anyway. As Keohane began having serious discussions with the athletic directors at Iowa, Iowa State and Utah, Krzyzewski made clear which direction he would like to see the search go. "There's nothing wrong with looking all over for the best possible person," he said, "but I think the best possible person is already right here."

With Krzyzewski, the most powerful person on campus, clearly endorsing Alleva, the outside candidates began pulling out. Keohane hired Alleva, who began upgrading the school's financial commitment to the football program, fired football coach Fred Goldsmith and planned renovations to Cameron Indoor Stadium.

Meanwhile, on the court, Krzyzewski's biggest problem entering the 1998-99 season seemed to be making sure all the former high school superstars on the roster weren't chafing under the constraints of having to fit into a system loaded with other superstars. Attrition had struck over the offseason as Mike Chappell, a 6-foot-8 sophomore from Michigan, transferred to Michigan State after seeing his role dwindle from starting forward to seldom-used reserve in the season's final weeks. Eight former high school All-Americans were coming back, and a ninth, 6'6" forward Corey Maggette, had enrolled for his freshman season. This would be delicate. Krzyzewski was ready.

"Each kid comes in on a different road," Krzyzewski said. "Some are ready to start, some need a little more time. It's about learning. You have two different paths you go. First there's the team path, and we have great kids, and they can see the importance of the team coming first. But second you have the individual path, and you have to have that, too. The two have to be compatible."

Everyone had their role. Elton Brand would be the center of the universe on offense, Battier the center of the universe on defense. Avery, who never started as a freshman, would run the offense. Langdon would be the primary perimeter option. Chris Carrawell would do just about anything and everything else, from slashing to the basket to clamping down on the opponent's top perimeter scorer. Maggette, Nate James and Burgess would have to be content coming off the bench. Senior center Taymon Domzalski, considered one of the top recruits ever from the state of New Mexico and a former freshman All-ACC pick, would have to be satisfied with helping Brand and Burgess get better in practice. Ridiculous, as Gillen said.

"If Taymon Domzalski played here, they'd build a monument to him on campus, right next to Thomas Jefferson," Gillen said. "There, he can't even get into the game. That's ridiculous."

How good Duke was in 1998-99 ... now that truly was ridiculous. The Blue Devils rampaged through the Atlantic Coast Conference like no team had ever done, becoming the first to go 16-0 in the conference, but more than that, winning those sixteen games by an average margin of 24.3 points. In all games, Duke's 26.1-point average winning margin was the seventh-highest ever in the NCAA. Duke entered the 1999 NCAA tournament with just one loss in thirty-three games, and the loss happened so late at night, so far away, and so early in the season, that by March it almost didn't seem real. The Blue Devils had lost 77-75 at the buzzer to Cincinnati in the Great Alaska Shootout back in November, the game starting after midnight, North Carolina time, and ending after 2 a.m. Even Cincinnati coach Bob Huggins was a little mystified at how his team had beaten the Blue Devils. "I'm not sure what happened, to tell you the truth," Huggins said.

The Blue Devils reached the Final Four in St. Petersburg, Florida, with the No. 1 ranking, a 36-1 record and the billing as one of the top teams of all time. The national media was ready to devour them. And every player was a great story.

Brand was the National Player of the Year who grew up so poor that his family, when he was a little baby, had to move in with relatives to avoid going homeless in Peekskill, New York. Given all that, Brand faced an enormous decision after the season: Leave Duke early for the NBA, or not? No Duke player had ever turned pro early. If he went, Brand would be the first. "I'm not thinking about it right now," he said during the tourna-ment. "I'm just thinking about Duke winning a national title."

Langdon was the fifth-year senior in his first Final Four, the only link, other than Krzyzewski, to that 13-18 Duke team in 1995. "I don't think there's been a kid in my program I've enjoyed knowing and following his progress more than Trajan," Krzyzewski said. "I've admired him tremendously. Remember back when you were eighteen, nineteen. I do, and I know there's no way I could have done the things he's done, handled the adversity he's handled. He's amazing."

Battier was the charge-taking, shot-blocking, ball-swiping defensive specialist who had emerged from his defensive cocoon to become an offensive threat in the final month of the season. He also was a former high school valedictorian who entertained the media with references to Shaolin monks and French art.

Carrawell was the inner-city kid from St. Louis who grew up playing money games in the neighborhood, one-on-one against someone else – anyone else – with as much as $1,000 of other people's money riding on the outcome. Carrawell was the one who, when Brand and Avery fouled out against St. John's in January and the game went into overtime, Krzyzewski pulled aside and said, "Where you go, we follow." Duke followed Carrawell to a 92-88 victory.

Avery was the point guard with the lost puppy look who almost didn't qualify for scholarship for academic reasons, who wanted to go to Duke but was told by Krzyzewski, after his high school junior season, that he didn't have the academic discipline to attend Duke. Avery emerged from that meeting in Krzyzewski's office to tell his mother, "I'm going to Duke." Now he was one of the best guards in the country, and, like Brand, considering leaving early for the NBA.

Even the bench was interesting. Nate James was the former Maryland prep star whose decision to attend Duke so enraged University of Maryland fans that, three years later, some of them picked a fight with James' family when Duke visited Cole Field House. Chris Burgess was the former No. 1 national recruit who had been given an overhaul by the Duke staff from forward to center and who was considering leaving after the season for a Mormon mission. The acrobatic Maggette was from the same ACC mold as David Thompson, Michael Jordan and Vince Carter, and although only a freshman reserve, already was considered by some NBA executives as the top pro prospect in the country.

And then there was Krzyzewski, back in the Final Four for the first time since 1994, since his back went out on him and the rest of his body followed suit in 1995, since he almost left Duke for Portland. After Duke beat Temple in the East regional final in East Rutherford, New Jersey, to advance to the Final Four, Krzyzewski looked up into the stands and blew kisses to his wife, Mickie, as he cut down his piece of the net. "We spent a lot of nights together when he questioned whether he could ever do it again," Mickie said, "whether it would be too hard for him, whether he would have what it takes to ever do it again. He knew he would be starting over."

"I've enjoyed this year as much as any year I've ever had," Krzyzewski said later. "Even if we don't win the national championship, I'll be able to look back and say I enjoyed the ride. Winning is important, but if that's all that matters, you're not looking at it the right way. Going through the things I went through helped me appreciate every moment of the journey you go through with these kids."

After the net was cut down, after the kisses were blown back and forth, after the rest of his team had run off the court and into the jubilant locker room, Mickie Krzyzewski shouted to her husband, "You've done it, Mike! You brought it back, and it's even better!"

Not quite. Duke stumbled in the Final Four, scratching out a 68-62 victory against an overmatched but defensively zealous Michigan State team in the semifinals, a victory that put the Blue Devils into the national championship game against Connecticut but left the cerebral Battier talking about "slippage."

"We suffered some slippage against Michigan State," Battier said the next day, "but I'm sure we'll get it back against Connecticut."

Or maybe not. The Huskies, the only team other than Duke to be ranked No. 1 at any point in the regular season, weren't afraid of the bully Blue Devils. Huskies guard Ricky Moore, a former high school teammate of Avery in Augusta, Georgia, blew past Avery throughout the first half and, at one point hopped up and down and shouted repeatedly to the Duke cheering section, "Can't guard me!" Connecticut forward Edmund Saunders knocked Brand to the floor after blocking his shot and loomed over him for a few seconds like a prize fighter relishing a knockout blow.

This battle had the most bitter of endings. There was Langdon, who had carried the doddering Blue Devils to the brink of the title with twenty-five points, trying to beat Moore one-on-one and traveling with thirteen seconds left and Duke trailing by one. There was Connecticut guard Khalid El-Amin making two free throws a few seconds later, pausing between the two foul shots to turn around and laugh in Avery's face. And there was Langdon again, the only senior contributor on this team, trying to hustle up the court for a last-gasp three-pointer to tie the game – and losing control of the ball, the game, the season and the dream. The final: Connecticut 77, Duke 74.

Afterward, as Avery sobbed on the court and Krzyzewski hugged him close, surrounded by celebrating Connecticut players and their fans, Langdon contemplated the worst part of all.

"I really wanted to win this for Coach K," he said. "He got us here. I just wanted to win it for him so bad."

EPILOGUE

It unraveled so fast, so unbelievably fast. Shane Battier might have called it slippage, his term for Duke's sub-par performance in the Final Four against Michigan State, but this wasn't slippage. This was a rock slide, the overnight erosion of the Duke basketball empire.

The emperor didn't take the erosion well.

Mike Krzyzewski, the coach who relates so well to his players, couldn't relate to this. Elton Brand was leaving for the NBA? OK, Krzyzewski could understand. Though only a sophomore, Brand was easily the best player in the country in 1998-99. His decision to turn professional was, as even Krzyzewski called it, a 'no-brainer.'

But William Avery? Corey Maggette? No, Krzyzewski could not relate to that at all. Avery, also a sophomore, decided to turn pro two days after assuring Krzyzewski he would be back for his junior season. Maggette, who started just three games as a freshman and averaged a modest 10.6 points per game but was an NBA talent, about that there was no question, kept Krzyzewski and everyone else guessing for nearly a month before declaring for the draft hours before the midnight May 16 deadline.

Brand had Krzyzewski's blessing to go to the NBA, so he got the first-class, royal-blue press conference at Cameron Indoor Stadium. Avery did not have Krzyzewski's blessing, so he did not get the royal blue sendoff. "Everyone is entitled to make their own decisions," Krzyzewski said in a statement, and then, plainly miffed, Krzyzewski made his own decision – no press conference for Avery.

By the time Maggette floored the Blue Devils by taking his basketball and his books and going home, Krzyzewski was stunned to silence. He issued no statement on Maggette's decision, his lack of response conveying his feelings quite loudly. Maggette had been booked on a flight from Chicago, his hometown, to Durham on May 15 to talk one last time with Krzyzewski, who planned to sell Maggette hard on the idea that another year at Duke would position Maggette into the first overall pick of the 2000 draft. No sale. The plane left O'Hare for Raleigh-Durham without Maggette, who had already decided not to come back.

With Maggette gone, Duke had lost five key players from its 37-2 team that reached the national title game. And only one, Trajan Langdon, was a senior. The exodus that saw Brand, Avery and Maggette go for the green also saw Brand's replacement, junior-to-be Chris Burgess, shock Krzyzewski in late April by choosing to transfer. By deciding so late to leave, Burgess effectively denied Krzyzewski the chance to recruit a pure center to replace him. "I am surprised by the decision and the timing of it," Krzyzewski said. "I certainly wish Chris and his family the best in the future."

Did you catch the little jab there? At Burgess' family?

That's who Duke people, for the most part, blamed. Ken Burgess, Chris' father, has long been accused of pulling the strings on his son's career, especially when Chris was in high school, when the family put out a two-page press release to announce his commitment to Duke. Since then Ken had been subtly prodding Chris toward leaving Duke, for two years at the least, to go on his Mormon mission. "He talks to me about it all the time," Chris said during the 1998-99 season. "He always tells me, 'Basketball will be there when you come back.'"

Brand, Avery, Maggette, Burgess. Four underclassmen, gone. And so was the assistant who helped recruit all of them, Quin Snyder, who in the middle of all this turnover also left for greener pastures, those in Columbia, Missouri, where he was hired as Missouri's next head basketball coach.

No, this wasn't slippage. This was a disaster. A possible starting five in 1999-2000 of Brand, Avery, Maggette, Chris Carrawell and Battier had become Battier, Carrawell and ... and ...

"It's kind of unbelievable," the mystified but still delightfully quotable Carrawell said in May. "I didn't think the whole gang wouldn't be back. We can't even play a pickup game. I'll be glad when the freshmen come in so we can play some pickup games."

Krzyzewski took two of the losses well. While he wasn't relishing the idea of losing Snyder from his staff, Krzyzewski had hoped for the past year that a program worthy of Snyder would believe Snyder, only thirty-two, was worthy of it. San Diego State wasn't worthy, Krzyzewski and Snyder felt, so Snyder withdrew his name from its hiring process about a month before taking the Missouri job. And while he wasn't eager to lose the services of Brand a full two years earlier than necessary, Krzyzewski knew in his heart the soft-spoken, athletically freakish 265-pound manchild was prepared for the NBA. "Elton is ready," Krzyzewski said in a statement released at Brand's press conference, where Brand sat on a royal blue dais in front of Duke basketball banners.

Duke did not give Avery a press conference. No, he had to rig one for himself, and he did it in his home town, not in Durham. He stood behind a temporary podium that, at the conclusion of the press conference, would go back to being a desk at the recreation center in Augusta, Georgia. Someone in the crowd was wearing a Duke hat. That was the Duke presence.

Someone asked Avery about Krzyzewski's seemingly harsh reaction to his decision to turn pro. "I think Coach K really loves me," Avery said. "He's got to do what he's got to do to protect his program."

Avery's decision left a peculiar taste in the mouth of everyone involved. It began when Krzyzewski, a few days before his surgery, told Avery he wanted a quick decision. "He said he would like an answer within a week," said Avery's mother, Terry Simonton, whose employment status – she was an electrician but had been unable to work the previous two years because of back problems – was a factor in her son's decision. "I don't know about you, but that sounded like it wasn't enough time for such a big decision. We weren't going to rush it."

After he and his mother met several times with Krzyzewski, Avery eventually decided to stay at Duke, and told Krzyzewski as much. A few days later, though, Brand had his on-to-the-NBA press conference, and Avery had a change of heart. He told Krzyzewski of his new decision that night. The next day, Krzyzewski issued his press release.

"I'm not in favor of William's decision at this time," Krzyzewski said. "We have done extensive research into the NBA for William and my conclusion was that entering the draft now would not be in his best interests. However, I certainly wish him the ultimate success in his future endeavors."

And what of Duke's endeavors? What of Krzyzewski?

Before the losses of Brand, Avery, Maggette and Burgess, Krzyzewski seemed to have his program cruising on auto pilot. He had brought in for the 1999-2000 season a recruiting class that rivaled the 1997 group. The latest haul included four national Top-10 players: 6-foot-11 forward Casey Sanders of Tampa, Florida; 6'2" point guard Jason Williams, the Parade National Player of the Year from Metuchen, New Jersey; 6'7" guard Michael Dunleavy of Portland, Oregon; and 6'9" forward Carlos Boozer of Juneau, Alaska, that state's first huge prospect since Trajan Langdon.

Even as he had that recruiting class in his pocket, but before Brand, Avery and company found the exit doors from Durham, Krzyzewski seemed to sense change was at hand, and that he might not be able to stop it. "We have the chance to stay up here among the elite, but it depends on what kids do, and how you recruit," Krzyzewski said. "Things are not as stable anymore. You have to constantly look at the way you're running your program and check for ways of making it as a stable as possible."

Three months after making that statement during the Final Four, Krzyzewski was sitting on the verandah of the exclusive Washington Duke Inn & Golf Club, not far from Cameron Indoor Stadium. In front of him was a spread of cold-cut sandwiches. On the putting green behind him were about twenty-five adolescent golfers, participating in Duke's summer golf camp. Everywhere else, it seemed, were media members.

This was Krzyzewski's first public appearance since the Final Four, since many of his best players had decided to leave for the NBA or another college. His media silence amid so much upheaval in the Duke program left one Raleigh columnist calling for Coach K to break his silence. Three weeks later, he did.

The first question was a cream puff. Someone with a microphone asked, "So, Coach, how's your hip?" Understand, Krzyzewski intimidates many members of the media.

Not all members, and not the core group of writers that covers him on a daily basis during the basketball season. But for almost everyone else, there is a level of intimidation, not necessarily one that Krzyzewski has tried to create. It just is. He is witty and frank and not worried about embarrassing someone for asking a silly or unnecessary question. And so, the first question posed to Krzyzewski, after all that had happened to Duke basketball, was about his new hip. (Came the answer: The hip was fine, thanks. Krzyzewski even proved it by bending over to tie his shoe – "showing off," as he jokingly called it.)

The press conference didn't get much more intense than that. Krzyzewski spent most of it lobbying for a committee to handle the day-to-day watchdogging of college basketball, a committee that currently doesn't exist within the NCAA. "Someone has to look out for college basketball," Krzyzewski said that day on the verandah, echoing a sentiment he had expressed over the past year. This time, though, Krzyzewski took it a step further. Whereas in the past he had expressed little concern over the number of players skipping out on college early for the NBA saying the game was bigger than this player or that player, on this day Krzyzewski asked for something to be done about the NBA issue – now that it had visited his program.

"It would be negligent for the people looking over our sport to not see this as a clear sign that something has to be done," he said. "You can't just keep losing players early (to the NBA) and not have an effect – on where they've left, and where they're going."

One week later, during the NBA draft, the three players who left Duke early were richly rewarded. Brand went first overall to the Chicago Bulls, his stock rising in the final weeks before the draft as his height proved indeed to be 6-foot-8, not 6'6" as some skeptics had predicted. Maggette and Avery also went in the first half of the first round, though Maggette's stock slipped even more than

Brand's rose after Maggette proved in workout after private workout with NBA teams that his perimeter shooting skills were lacking. Maggette went 13th overall to Seattle, which then traded him to Orlando. Avery went 14th to the Minnesota Timberwolves. Meanwhile, Langdon also went high, going 11th overall to Cleveland, making Duke the first team in history to have four first-rounders.

It was quite an achievement for a program built twenty years earlier from the ashes of past greatness by Krzyzewski. But it left him looking to rebuild, looking to replace his top assistant and recruiter (Snyder), his most dominant player since Grant Hill (Brand), his rapidly improving point guard (Avery), plus young talents Maggette and Burgess.

Not to mention his hip.

———

COACH K'S CAREER RECORD

Year	School	Overall W/L	ACC W/L	Notes
1976	Army	11-14		
1977	Army	20-8		
1978	Army	19-9		NIT Tournament
1979	Army	14-11		
1980	Army	9-17		
1981	Duke	17-13	6-8 (T5)	NIT Tournament
1982	Duke	10-17	4-10 (T6)	
1983	Duke	11-17	3-11(7)	
1984	Duke	24-10	7-7 (T3)	NCAA Tournament
1985	Duke	23-8	8-6 (T4)	NCAA Tournament
1986	Duke	37-3	12-2 (1)	NCAA Final Four-Runnerup
1987	Duke	24-9	9-5 (3)	NCAA Tournament
1988	Duke	28-7	9-5 (3)	NCAA Final Four
1989	Duke	28-8	9-5 (T2)	NCAA Final Four
1990	Duke	29-9	9-5 (2)	NCAA Final Four-Runnerup
1991	Duke	32-7	11-3 (1)	NCAA Final Four-Champion
1992	Duke	34-2	14-2 (1)	NCAA Final Four-Champion
1993	Duke	24-8	10-6 (T3)	NCAA Tournament
1994	Duke	28-6	12-4 (1)	NCAA Final Four-Runnerup
1995	Duke	9-3	0-1	Out after back surgery
1996	Duke	18-13	8-8 (T4)	NCAA Tournament
1997	Duke	24-9	12-4 (1)	NCAA Tournament
1998	Duke	32-4	15-1 (1)	NCAA Tournament
1999	Duke	37-2	16-0 (1)	NCAA Final Four-Runnerup

Career Record: 542-214 (.717) -24 years
Duke Record: 469-155 (.752) -19 years
NCAA Tournament Record: 48-13 (.787) -15 years

DUKE'S RECORD UNDER COACH K

Year	Overall W/L	ACC W/L	ACC Tourn. Finish	AP Poll
1980-81	17-13	6-8 (T5th)	Quarterfinalist	
1981-82	10-17	4-10 (T6th)	Quarterfinalist	
1982-83	11-17	3-11 (7th)	Quarterfinalist	
1983-84	24-10	7-7 (T3rd)	Finalist	14th
1984-85	23-8	8-6 (T4th)	Semifinalist	10th
1985-86	37-3	12-2 (1st)	Champion	1st
1986-87	24-9	9-5 (3rd)	Quarterfinalist	17th
1987-88	28-7	9-5 (3rd)	Champion	5th
1988-89	28-8	9-5 (T2nd)	Finalist	9th
1989-90	29-9	9-5 (2nd)	Quarterfinalist	15th
1990-91	32-7	11-3 (1st)	Finalist	6th
1991-92	34-2	14-2 (1st)	Champion	1st
1992-93	24-8	10-6 (T3rd)	Quarterfinalist	10th
1993-94	28-6	12-4 (1st)	Semifinalist	6th
1994-95*	13-18	2-14 (9th)	Quarterfinalist	
1995-96	18-13	8-8 (T4th)	Quarterfinalist	
1996-97	24-9	12-4 (1st)	Quarterfinalist	8th
1997-98	32-4	15-1 (1st)	Finalist	3rd
1998-99	37-2	16-0 (1st)	Champion	1st

*out after back surgery, only coached
the first 12 games of the season.

Coaches Poll	Postseason Results	Captains
	NIT	Gene Banks, Kenny Dennard
		Vince Taylor
		Tom Emma, Chip Engelland
14th	NCAA Second Round	Richard Ford, Doug McNeely
12th	NCAA Second Round	Jay Bryan, Dan Meagher
1st	NCAA Finalist	Johnny Dawkins, David Henderson
	NCAA Sweet Sixteen	Tommy Amaker
5th	NCAA Semifinalist	Billy King, Kevin Strickland
7th	NCAA Semifinalist	Danny Ferry, Quin Snyder
14th	NCAA Finalist	Robert Brickey
6th	NCAA Champion	Clay Buckley, Greg Koubek
1st	NCAA Champion	Brian Davis, Christian Laettner
10th	NCAA Second Round	Thomas Hill, Bobby Hurley
6th	NCAA Finalist	Marty Clark, Grant Hill, Antonio Lang Kenny Blakeney, Erik Meek, Cherokee Parks
	NCAA First Round	Jeff Capel, Chris Collins
8th	NCAA Second Round	Jeff Capel, Greg Newton, Carmen Wallace
5th	NCAA Elite Eight	Trajan Langdon, Roshown McLeod, Steve Wojciechowski
1st	NCAA Finalist	Trajan Langdon

ABOUT THE AUTHOR

Gregg Doyel has covered ACC basketball for *The Charlotte Observer* since November, 1997. Before that he was at *The Miami Herald*, where he covered the Florida Marlins from 1995-1997. He has gone from writing about game seven of the World Series, which the Marlins won in eleven innings, to writing about an ACC basketball season that had Duke ranked No. 1 and North Carolina ranked No. 2. Since then, he has followed the Duke team for two seasons, including its 37-2 team that made it all the way to the 1999 championship game.

Doyel is a graduate of the University of Florida and is a member of the Atlantic Coast Sports Writers Association. He currently resides in Apex, North Carolina, with his wife, Melody, and their two sons, Macon and Jackson.

PHOTO CREDITS